From Pain to Praise

The Prose and Poems of a Daughter-in-Process

INACENT SAUNDERS

Copyright © 2015 Inacent Saunders

Timothy's Tribe Publications, Brooklyn, New York

All rights reserved. This book or any portion thereof may not be reproduced or used in any manner whatsoever without the express written permission of the publisher except for the use of brief quotations in a book review. For permission requests, send an email to the publisher at admin@inacentsaunders.com.

ISBN: 069246980X
ISBN-13: 978-0692469804

FIRST EDITION

One Thing Remains
Written by Brian Johnson, Jeremy Riddle, Christa Black Gifford
© 2010 Bethel Music Publishing (ASCAP)/Mercy Vineyard Publishing (ASCAP) (Admin by Music Services, Inc.)/Christajoy Music (BMI)(Christa Black is admin. by Bethel Music Publishing). All rights reserved. Used by permission.

Scripture quotations noted The Message are taken from The Message. Copyright © 1993, 1994, 1995, 1996, 2000, 2001, 2002. Used by permission of NavPress Publishing Group

Scripture quotations noted NIV are taken from THE HOLY BIBLE, NEW INTERNATIONAL VERSION®, NIV® Copyright © 1973, 1978, 1984, 2011 by Biblica, Inc.® Used by permission. All rights reserved worldwide.

Scripture quotations marked ESV are from the ESV® Bible (The Holy Bible, English Standard Version®), copyright © 2001 by Crossway, a publishing ministry of Good News Publishers. Used by permission. All rights reserved.

Scripture quotations marked BBE are from the Bible in Basic English which is in the Public Domain. The Bible In Basic English was printed in 1965 by Cambridge Press in England.

DEDICATION

This book is dedicated in memory of my Grand-Aunt, Muriel Boyce, affectionately called Aunt Mu. In her younger years she was known for her sharp tongue. Despite that, or perhaps because of that, she was the very expression of love. And as the matriarch of the family, she ensured we stayed connected with one another. As she aged, I saw her grow in relationship with God. And as she transformed, she coincidentally became a picture of a "Daughter-in-Process", a true inspiration. Aunt Mu took her flight in 2011, but I am eternally grateful for the lessons I learned from her – especially her final one: that the process never ends. As one of her favorite singers would sing "Everything must change." And every step of the journey is absolutely worth it.
Rest in Peace Aunt Mu.

CONTENTS

Acknowledgements	i
Introduction	1
Daughter-in-Process	5
But Will Tomorrow Ever Come	8
Guilt	16
He Heals the Brokenhearted	21
Heartbreak	51
The Release	54
Le the Wall Come Down	56
I'm Sorry	59
I Was Born to Serve You	67
My Father's Father	74
From a Daughter's Vacation Journal	79
Identity Cry-Sis	84
It's Not Love, if It's Hate	90
Love, Like, or Lust	91
Will You Carry My Son?	96
The Miscarriage	99
Grief	106
Unlock God's Thoughts Toward You	108
Stay on the Potter's Wheel	111
For Every Mountain (My Testimony)	114

ACKNOWLEDGMENTS

To Daddy **God**, I love you Lord, with all I am. My life's story would have come to an end years ago had you not stepped in, right on time. I thank You for having a plan and a purpose for my life, even before I was born.

To my **mom Sheila**, you are the maverick that raised me! You taught me so much in life. Your outspoken character is so far from mine, but I smile with pride when I open my mouth and hear your boldness – your voice – come out. You taught me to count my blessings, every day. And you will forever be the smartest lady in the world to me.

To my **sister Irene**, you're my number one cheerleader and biggest supporter in life. I already know that you will be among the first to purchase this book. You fostered every interest I had in childhood by providing tools for me to learn and explore. Because of you, I've always believed that I could reach the stars.

To my **extended family**, thank you for your prayers and patience as I struggled through my adolescence. If you did judge me through the many mistakes I made, I never knew it. I only ever knew and felt your love, without which, I would have been even more lost than I already was.

To my **friends**, you loved me even when I didn't feel worthy of love. We've comforted each other through life's losses, and celebrated one another through its joys. Whenever we gather from the far places we now call home, it's as if we were never apart. Thank you for being real friends.

If it had not been for all of you, I would have never made it… *from pain to praise.*

INTRODUCTION

Adolescence was a rocky time for me, as it is for many. It was at this stage in life that Satan made it clear that he desired to kill me. That might be considered strong or dramatic language to some, but scripture certainly says that he has come but to steal, kill and destroy. And I can testify that he certainly tried me. So I did what most people do, I self-medicated. The various vices I took on to try to heal the pain included chain smoking, abusive drinking, fornicating and excessive partying. But the one healthy coping mechanism I clung to was writing.

I've always loved writing. And during adolescence I was no stranger to using poetry and short stories to tell the tales I did not dare to speak out loud. However, in my late teens, I discovered and fell in love with spoken word poetry. After seeing the likes of Jessica Care Moore and Saul Williams performing on late night TV shows and starring in independent films, I made my first trip to the Nuyorican Poet's Café at age 19. I remember pressing my way through the crowd and perching myself on the too-skinny, too-hard, metal rung of a ladder off against a wall with a friend from college. We stayed and listened to hours of performers. I was in heaven. I began to write spoken word pieces as a form of release and I would only share them in intimate circles, if so led. In any event, as time went on, life became harder, and the temptations of the world grew stronger, my spoken word pieces became more and more explosive. It got so bad that when I would reread my finished pieces, I couldn't believe the anger, lust and pain that had been pent up inside of me. In fact, there was more than anger, there was rage. There was more than lust, there was perversion. There was more than pain, there was trauma. My writing became a thermometer of what was going on inside of me. And more often than not, it was burning hot.

From Pain to Praise: The Prose and Poems of a Daughter-in-Process is a personal anthology of poems, journal entries, and other writings that were written over the past 15 years of my life. Although each piece reflects my mindset at the time it was written, my pre-rebirth (before I rededicated my life to Christ) pieces are more emotionally tumultuous. But throughout my process of becoming a child of God – A "Daughter" of The King – I've realized that the tragedy of a life lived "in Christ" is that although we have a Savior to turn our burdens over to, life is still hard. Life is still filled with moments of pain. However, I've also come to learn that the beauty of a life lived in Christ is that with him, there is joy, peace, and understanding in the midst of the trials of life. That's what I mean by "From Pain to Praise". My life did not suddenly become devoid of trouble when I got born again – which is what we sometimes lead non-believers to think. But a life in Christ enables me to praise Him even in the midst of trouble.

The pieces in this book are not presented in any particular order. I tried to group them together in such a way that there was a natural progression of themes, however there are no clearly defined chapters or sections. To this end, the reader should not expect there to be a chronological flow to the writing. Some of the themes that will emerge are that of identity, relationships, and love. But one will not know what's coming "next" once they finish any given piece. In essence, each piece stands alone.

As I compiled this collection, I flinched at some of the raw emotion expressed in my earlier pieces. In fact, I questioned whether or not I should even include some of the pieces. I knew that some of my readers (particularly my Christian audience) might take issue with the use of the explicit and profane language. However, the assignment I was given by God was to let this book be a testimony of truth, MY TRUTH.

So, what is MY TRUTH?

The truth is I was once in a lot of pain.

The truth is this pain was reflected not only in my actions, but in my thoughts and thus my writing as well.

The truth is I did not always know how to bridle my tongue.

The truth is I did not always have the joy and peace of Christ.

The truth is there are times, even now, when my emotions take me back to those places of hurt, and some of the pieces written before I was saved might actually reflect my current feelings and thoughts.

The truth is I am not a perfect person, and there are no perfect people.

The truth is people don't just need the whitewashed version of our testimonies. They need to know that Christians really do understand their pain. And if they know that, then maybe they'll understand our praise, and perhaps find some of their own. My prayer is that this book will help someone examine their own truth, and in doing so, seek the God that can guide them on their own journey – from pain to praise.

DAUGHTER-IN-PROCESS

Morning reflections...

Yesterday I had a conversation with my sisters Shon and Raven about being "in process" with God. This morning, Raven posted about the topic as well. And as recently as Saturday I had a conversation with Lyddia about it. I said to her, "I'm in process. Deep process. But, I feel like I'm always in process." I was a bit overwhelmed. "Well", she said, "You are. But that's just you, Inacent." Yes, always in process, and always "processing" (reflecting on and coming into understanding of) whatever it is I'm going through. In 5 years the process has never stopped. There have been times of slow progress, largely due to lack of faith. Then there have been times in which I've allowed Him to do the QUICK WORK He said He could. Either way, the process has NEVER stopped. For that I am grateful. Why? Because it's what makes me who I am! LITERALLY, the process is MAKING me.

I remember when He gave me a vision of the woman I would become. I remember crying REAL TEARS; not trusting God that it could happen. I remember asking "Who IS that woman?!? What kind of cruel joke is this? That could never be me!" Well, I'm not completely her yet. But I'm closer than ever before. So much so, that now I find myself looking BACK on my life and asking, "Who WAS that woman? What kind of false existence was I living? That was NEVER the real me!"   But I tell you this: regardless of who I was in the past, or who I'll be in the future, I – for the first time ever in life – am in LOVE with the woman I am NOW. This is not conceit. This is self-awareness. I know who I am. I know my purpose. I know Who I serve. And I LOVE ME. I love me, FIERCELY. Just like my God loves me – FIERCELY!

My prayer today is that for those "in process", that they love themselves enough to let it happen, and that they fall in love with the process. ALL OF IT:

- The experiences in the mountain AND the valley
- The fun parts and the uncomfortable parts
- The times you have to walk the line alone AND the times you have to engage in corporate seeking and accountability.

Fall in love with the chastening (correction) of God. In Hebrews 12 we are reminded that God corrects us because He loves us. And without His correction, we're not REALLY His children. Let Him make you into the Sons and Daughters that He predestined you to be, EVEN before the world began. Have enough faith to say:

- "There is more for me to have, and I will obtain it."
- "There is more for me to do, and I will accomplish it."
- "There is more for me to BE, and I will BECOME it."

Stand on faith today. And know that your God, who loves you FIERCELY, is not content to let you stay in your current condition.

"There has never been the slightest doubt in my mind that the God who started this great work in you would keep at it and bring it to a flourishing finish on the very day Christ Jesus appears." Philippians 1:6 (*The Message*)

Stay in process!

BUT WILL TOMORROW EVER COME

Sometimes, I feel like the world forgot about me,
My father didn't want me,
My mother don't even know me,
and God never did like me.

The world just forgot about me.
My own image I hardly see.
Long hair
Slim in the waist
6 feet tall
With the perfect face
kills me!
Naomi Campbell
Tyra Banks
And what? I'm supposed to say thanks?!
For what?
Just 'cuz you took 2 sistahs,
tightened their weaves,

covered their big ol' foreheads,
gave 'em tig ol' bitties,
and slapped their pictures on the cover of Elle
(so that *The African American image is celebrated as well*)??
Fuck that!
'Cuz that ain't me!
I mean it's too many sisters that don't match their "beauty".
But I tell you something else: we're faaaar from ugly!!!!
That shit irks me!
I mean, when they gon' stop selling that same sorry story?
I love Ms. Monique Parker with her big sexy confidence.
I love Ms. Badu and her dangerous fashion sense.
I love Ms. Kelly Price with her big voice singing elegance.
I love Ms. Lauren hill, with her locks and
♫ "If IIIII RULED the WORLD…" ♪
Yeah, what *if* we ruled the world Lauren?

Man I tell you,
Sometimes, I feel like the world forgot about me,
My father didn't want me,
My mother don't even know me,
and God never did like me.

My father didn't want me.
He made that clear the day he walked out.
He never looked back, 'cuz if he had

He woulda heard me shout:
BASTARD!
IRRESPONSIBLE!
NO GOOD!
UNCARING!
PIECE of – me…
P-E-A-C-E of me
Daddy…
Why??
Where were you when I graduated
the first, second and third time?
Where were you when I was applying to schools
and couldn't make up my mind?
Where were you when I went to prom
in my beautiful, pure white dress?
Where were you when I was under
all that GOD DAMN STRESS?!?!
Where were you when I dropped out of school
and everything stopped for me, including time?
Where were you when I was suffering from depression
and pretended that everything was fine?
Counselor-lady said, "Inacent, There's something missing in your life."
NO SHIT, MISS!
But, I digress…
After all,
My feelings of inappropriateness,
of nothingness,
of hopelessness,
and copelessness

had nothing to do with him.
Or did they?
Do they?
I don't know.
But HEY, I do know that I suffer from a slight syndrome called...
Well I don't know what it's called.
But it should be called
"DaddysLittleGirlFeelin'LikeDaddyWishesSheWasNeverBorn-AndDoesntCareThatSheEverWas"
Syndrome -
Complex A for Abandonment, or
B for Banishment, or
C for Cheap, or
D for too Damn Deep
to talk about right now.
So forget it.
It takes too much energy to hate you.
I know somebody here relates... do you?
Anyway, you been gone so long
and missed so much,
it'd take all night just to talk about
how you didn't love me enough.

Man I tell you,
Sometimes, I feel like the world forgot about me,
My father didn't want me,
My mother don't even know me,
and God never did like me.

My mother don't even know me.

She asks me all these questions.
Does she see a true reflection?
"You was drinking, wasn't you?"
"You smoking weed?"
"Who you fuckin?"
"You tried that xtasy"
Damn!
For a woman to name her child Inacent,
she sure don't believe I'm living up to it.
She just so busy conjuring up the negative
she never takes the time to recognize the positive.
Just once I'd like to hear
"I'm so proud."
"I'm so happy!"
"I Love you."
Yeah, we don't use that word in my house... Love.
Kisses and hugs
are reserved for Christmas and birthdays.
Over at my homegirl's house they use it EVERYday.
I mean, I know I'm loved, but sometimes it's nice to hear it too.
People, mostly women, tell their lovers that all the time –
That they wanna hear "I Love You" once in a while.
Would it be too much for a child to ask the same?
Or maybe even once in a while, could you not forget my name?
But instead of open arms, I usually get a cold shoulder.
Instead of recognition, I get nothing but doubt.

FROM PAIN TO PRAISE

It's hard to express my feelings about my mother.
I guess everyone thinks their parents are lacking in one department or another.
My mom did her best to provide.
I just wish that she could have stood by my side –
more often.
I would have taken a hug, over a toy any day.
A kiss over a new shirt or a chance to go out and play.
A gleam of recognition over almost anything else
I would have felt
so much more loved.

Man I tell you,
Sometimes, I feel like the world forgot about me,
My father didn't want me,
My mother don't even know me,
and God never did like me.

God never did like me
If he did, how could he do this to me?
Day after day, I see the world coming apart.
And day after day I feel my heart breaking apart.
Sisters:
Tricking
Shooting
Sniffing and snorting
Gold-digging
Ride or die bitches.
I guess they never realized that by riding they *were* dying.

Putting more value on trying to get that pair of designer jeans,
then on the value of their unborn baby, and their unborn baby's dreams.
Brothers:
Baby making
Life taking
Drug dealing
Paper chasin'
Just "chillin' like a villain"
Weed smoking
Gun toting
What? Soldiers???
Who they protecting?
Not my community.
Whose honor are they defending?
Not mine or my families.
Who are they at war with?
Looks like each other
But what war are they fighting?
Aint no war, they just some niggas dying!
But it hurts!
They don't see their worth on this earth.
Black people dying from the time of their birth.

Y'all ever stop and think like this?
You ever get fed up with this shit?
Don't tell me you don't,
'Cuz Then you'd be living a lie.
What one does affects us all
I KNOW you're not blind.

I wake up each morning and I'm engulfed in all this emotion.
And I'm confronted with the reality
that it may be up to me to set the wheels in motion.
What wheels?
The wheels of change…
To make a better world so no one feels forgotten.
To bear a son who can be true father, so his daughter feels wanted.
To be a mother who knows her children,
So maybe more people will feel truly loved by HIM!

'Cuz Man I tell you,
Sometimes, I feel like the world forgot about me,
My father didn't want me,
My mother don't even know me,
and God never did like me.

But Maybe I'll feel different tomorrow.

GUILT

I let them mount me.
From any direction they choose.
No foreplay,
Just penetrate,
'Cuz I feel I have nothing left to lose.
It's dry down there.
It
hurts
every time.
But I pay it no mind,
And just force my hips to grind.

I moan and
Groan and
Cry out as if enjoying he,
All the while
thinking
"How fucked up can I be?"

FROM PAIN TO PRAISE

Oh yeah, that's right,
I'm plenty fucked up!
To do this I make sure I'm in an
Absolute haze
Or a
Hypnotic daze
Before I even think about giving it up.

And at some point in my drunken stupor,
I realize I'm doing that thing again.
And in my mind I start to curse.

What thing?
Well, I need to feel punished when I spread my legs,
So I make sure he gives it to me good.
How?

First I
Drink too much making sure
I feel the shame of overindulgence.

Then I
Leave with a man
Of my own choosing,
Seizing
that one brief moment of power.

Next I
Talk shit the whole ride to his place,
Prepping him by pumping his aggression.
(And yes, I did say his place 'cuz unfamiliar

surroundings make me feel that much more vulnerable.)

After that I
Shower.
It won't be right,
If it aint tight
and clean
Like it was when untouched.

Then I
Coyly get on the bed.
But I don't want no gentle love making,
Only penetration with hard, violent thrusts.

And right about then,
The disgust sets in…
In me
As he thrusts
In me
And out
And in
No sin…
In this.
I scream like I'm enjoying this.
He don't realize that at that point
I tighten the punany
Wanting to feel more agony.
The extasy
Is not in this.
Pump harder

and harder
Don't stop.
Cum
Collapse
on top...
With a grunt
This cunt
has been sufficiently tortured.
Mission accomplished.
Nut bust
And all my trust
in men
Still
Nonexistent.

A flood of guilt and insecurity
would then overwhelm me.
But this is how it was
Regularly...
A loss of pride,
slowed
sex drive...
Not wanting it if it felt good.
Don't know what good feel like
Only torn pussy
Ripped walls
Bleeding
Faking
Smiling

I want so badly to feel the way that I did,

when I was still a virgin.
But back then
The prospective joy of sex was taken
By
Unwelcome hands grabbing,
Unwelcome hands touching,
Unwelcome hands covering... My mouth...
Their mouths?
Their mouths were usually smiling.
Now, mine was smiling.
Smiling that same smile they did,
cuz now I could.
My mouth isn't covered.
I smile for the times that I couldn't,
Even though this time I actually shouldn't.
And I fear
that it will always be this way.

HE HEALS THE BROKENHEARTED

Part 1

It was 6:12am. Sandra stared sleepily, yet intently, into the mirror. She checked her face for any new blemishes, enlarged pores, and stray chin hairs that seemed to spring up overnight. The older she got, the more seemed to spring up. She also checked for the general shape of her face. She rubbed her petite hand over her mostly smooth brown skin. Was it rounder today? Was her chin more or less angular? Was there a double chin trying to reemerge? She wasn't fanatical about her weight, but having at one time been much heavier, and having gone through ups and downs in her weight, she had learned to watch the shape of her face as an indicator of the necessity to perhaps cut back on calories or increase her physical activity. Her face seemed to tell a better story than her waist, so this worked for her.

This morning routine was also her way of mentally preparing for the day. Sandra had learned that if she could face herself in the morning, literally, she could face the world that day. And if there was something she saw that she didn't like about herself, or if her mind was flooded with early morning negative commentary, as it sometimes was, she would quickly spout some positive self-talk to get her mind into a better place. She refused to step out of her house feeling "less than". She had lived way too many years of her life that way - her entire adolescence in fact. And all it had gotten her was a history of panic disorder, low self-esteem, and a drinking problem to self-medicate. Now at the threshold of age 35, she had overcome all of these things, much of it by the power of self-awareness.

Sandra held self-awareness in high regard. In fact, she described it as one of the most sacred things in life. Every level of self-awareness she had achieved only led her to becoming more and more of her "most authentic self". She had a sort of fascination with the concept. Since the days she had gone through cognitive behavioral therapy to help her deal with her panic disorder, she had learned the value of "self-reflection", "introspection" and "presence of mind". These words weren't just shrink-talk to her. She got it! It worked! And so she worked it. She worked it so well that she had come to believe that self-awareness was the key to living one's best life possible. To this end, she didn't start a single day without at least a few moments of self-reflection. Today was no different. She also didn't go a single week without her regular visit to Jackie, her longtime therapist who initially treated her for panic disorder – an appointment she'd be keeping later on today.

After her bathroom mirror routine, Sandra grabbed her bible, turned on a single lamp above her living room couch, and comfortably curled up for her morning devotions. She was a Christian, saved for seven years now, and tried not to let a day go by without reflecting on at least a few scriptures. When she first got saved, she was way more diligent about this. Now, not so much. But she had at least 30 minutes to spare this morning before getting ready for work. She opened her Bible to the book of Jeremiah and her eyes fell on a highlighted scripture. It read "'For I know the plans I have for you,' declares the Lord, 'plans to prosper you and not to harm you, plans to give you hope and a future.'" (Jeremiah 29:11, NIV). It was a familiar passage of scripture that she often found solace in. It reminded her that God was concerned about her future and intended for her to be successful. This reassurance was necessary to Sandra's psychic health. In her former life, it seemed as if success was never to be obtained. So knowing that the God she served was rooting for her and planning for her success was major! But on this particular morning, this scripture didn't fill Sandra with the hope it usually did. In being forced to consider her future, her mind wandered over to her past. Not the past of drinking and partying, but further back, to her childhood. So much of her fragility was based on the experiences of her childhood. One of which, involved her father, whom she hadn't seen since the age of 7. And she blamed herself for his disappearance.

Sandra stared blankly out of her living room window. The curtains were mostly drawn, only allowing the slightest bit of daylight in. Rain fell lightly against the window as she stared out past her bushes, past her driveway, past her neighbor's home across the street, into the past. She remembered the last day she saw her father. Her heart picked up in pace, if only for a moment, as she recalled the last look she saw on his face, a look she put there. She saw herself standing there, in the afterschool program, behind her desk, visibly confused one moment, then after a glint of clarity, utter anguish overshadowed her heart, although her face never showed it. She didn't even speak of this incident until she was a teenager. For nearly 10 years that image of herself tormented her. When she would recall it, that tormented child reawakened inside of her, wanting to express that anguish she felt so many years prior. But every time the memory came back, Sandra just buried it deeper into her subconscious. But here she was, nearly middle aged, and the secure place she tried to keep this memory buried was bursting at the seams. It wouldn't be contained much longer. Nor should it. She'd have to deal with this – soon.

Sandra's father and mother were never married. In fact, Sandra's Dad was married to another woman when he and her mom conceived her. Yes, she was the product of adultery. Oddly, she was never really bothered by that fact. She was keenly aware that had her mom and dad not given into whatever desires they had for each other, she would not even exist. How could she be mad at that? Anyway, she had only ever had a few phone conversations and received a few Merry Birthday gifts from her dad during her childhood years. (Being a December baby, Sandra was used to receiving a single gift from people that would double as both a Christmas and Birthday gift. She was never bothered by it, but she called them her "Merry Birthday" gifts.) And since he was married, and his wife was not the least bit pleased with the thought of an outside child borne out of adultery, Sandra barely ever saw her dad. It was so bad, she couldn't pick him out of a line up if she needed to. But she knew he loved her. Her mom always stressed how much he loved her. And she believed it. She knew it. And she loved him. But the daddy/daughter relationship is no different than any other relationship. No matter how much love there might be, once a heart's been broken, things can never be the same. And so, Sandra's dad went from sporadic phone calls, occasional visits and annual obligatory Merry Birthday gifts, to nothing at all. Sandra knew the exact moment she broke her daddy's heart.

Sandra shook her head to bring herself back into

the present moment. Her devotional time was almost over. Instead of reaffirming herself, her mental trip down memory lane left her feeling weaker than when she started. If God's plans were truly to prosper her, she had to get free from the restraints of her past. She ended her morning devotion by getting on her knees and praying carefully aloud.

> *"Almighty God, Creator of heaven and earth, He who holds the world in His hands, I thank You for giving me another day of life, another day to serve You, another day to live the abundant life Your Son Jesus promised. Lord, You know that as I read Your Word this morning, that bitter root was exposed again. That root of shame and guilt concerning my father. I'm ready Lord. I'm ready to deal with this issue. I want to be set free from guilt and shame. No more confusion. No more pain. No more 'what ifs'. I can't live with the 'what ifs' anymore. I can only deal with what is. I wanna live in the present, no longer in the past. Help me please. Give me strength. Give me clarity. Heal my heart. Give me closure. I'm ready for this journey. It's necessary. I trust and pray that You will do a quick work in this*

matter. In Jesus' name I pray, Amen."

Sandra got up off her knees with tears in her eyes. She wiped them away with her hands, and went back to the bathroom, examining her face in the mirror one last time before she hopped in the shower.

Part 2

It was 12:30 p.m. and Sandra was running from her office to make her appointment with Jackie on time. She made it through her morning meetings unbothered, but was now ready to do some digging. The trip across town usually took about 20 minutes if she walked briskly, so she was confident she'd make it in time. As she passed the store fronts she'd occasionally glance over to see her reflection in the glass. A single passing glance would signal her to pick her head up, straighten out her back, adjust the limp she had from the bunion that throbbed on her left foot. She made it to Jackie's office and was greeted by the receptionist, Catherine. Catherine was pleasant enough. She never made mindless chit-chat which Sandra was grateful for. But she made sure that the waiting room was always comfortable and clean – something else Sandra was grateful for. After waiting in silence for about 5 minutes, Jackie buzzed Catherine, instructing her to let Sandra in. "Jackie's ready for you Sandra." "Alright, thanks." Sandra replied as she gathered her belongings and made her way into Jackie's office. Once inside, she sat down in the high backed, brown leather armchair with a sigh.

Jackie looked Sandra in the eyes and smiled. "Hi Sandra".
"Hi Jackie." Sandra replied.
"How are you today?"
"I'm well for the most part. Could always be better." Sandra replied with a smile and light chuckle.
"So… what's on your mind today?"
Sandra was a bit surprised that Jackie was getting right down to new business. Sometimes she'd start by following up on the previous weeks' conversation. But today, she was moving right along. She paused, allowing Sandra some time to gather her thoughts. "Well," Sandra began, "I've been thinking about my Dad again."
"Oh? Really? What about him?"
Sandra was slightly annoyed that Jackie asked this question. She knew what this was about. Although Sandra had not yet shared the whole story with Jackie, she knew enough to know that *the incident* plagued her memory. "You know… That episode from my childhood that I've mentioned," said Sandra.
"Yes, you've mentioned it a few times. Would you like to talk about that today? Do you think you're ready?" Jackie's manner was gentle, but matter of fact. She had an appropriate balance of emotion and tone when she spoke. Sandra admired that about her.
"Yea… I think I'm ready."

"Okay. So you can begin however and wherever you think it would be most helpful."

Sandra paused for a moment, staring up at a painting that Jackie had hanging in her office. It was some sort of old medieval town scenery, with people hustling and bustling about their business. They were dressed in clothing that you might see peasants during that era wearing. Some were busy tending to animals, some stood in small circles socializing or discussing business, or so it would seem. Others waved to each other from across the way. There was one gentleman in the painting that Sandra often focused in on. He was bending over a barrel of some type of goods, digging them out several at a time with some sort of ladle. Years ago, Sandra noticed that she'd focus on this particular character in this painting whenever she was being thoughtful, searching her mind for an answer to some question that Jackie had posed to her. One day, she mentioned to Jackie how she caught herself doing that, and if she had any idea why? Jackie said she couldn't say for sure, but that perhaps as Sandra tried to dig out and sort through her own emotions and thoughts, it was helpful to look at this character that was doing something very similar. Sandra thought that was possibly one of the deepest, most insightful things she had ever heard. That was the day she decided to keep Jackie as her therapist. Sandra stared at her little man in the painting as she began to share.

"My father was never a major part of my life. He

came by, as far as I could remember, maybe twice a year or so. There were occasional phone calls but those weren't very eventful. And with my mother and sister being such integral parts of my life, I never understood the 'purpose' of a father. Although I knew he loved me, and I loved him, I honestly didn't understand his role in my life. Anyway, one day, at the age of 7 or so, I was at the afterschool program that operated on the ground floor of my apartment building. A man came and stood in the doorway, and just stared at me. He looked kinda familiar, but I couldn't place where I knew him from. The teacher caught him staring and said 'Excuse me sir, is there someone you know here?' He said, with a smile, 'Yeah, that little girl riiiiight there.' and he pointed at me. The teacher turned to me and said 'Inacent, do you know this man?'"

"Well did you?" Jackie broke in. (That was unlike her.)

"That's just it; the lightbulb of recognition wouldn't come fast enough in my head. So I just slowly shook my head and said 'No'. That's when it happened."

"What happened?" Jackie broke in again.

"I saw it. We looked at each other dead in the eyes and I swear I saw it. I watched it happen."

"What did you see Sandra?"

Sandra took her eyes off of the painting, looked Jackie in the eye, and with tears in her own eyes she said, "I saw his heart break."

Sandra began to sob internally. She kept her

composure for the most part but her chest tightened and her eyes filled with a well of tears that threatened to burst forth like a flood if she said another word. Her breathing became a bit shallow for a second. All of her senses seemed to heighten in a single instant, and then slowly began to level off. Sandra realized she hadn't taken another breath since her confession. So she gasped heavily. And in her next breath she gently cried, "Jackie! I broke my father's heart!"

Jackie looked at Sandra compassionately and gently asked "So, you think that man was your father?"

Sandra whispered "I know he was. I realized it too late, but it was. When I said 'no', I remember the look of utter rejection and pain on his face. But it was his eyes. I saw his heart break as I looked into his eyes. It was then, that I realized that man was my father."

Jackie was silent for a few moments. Then she asked "What happened next?"

"Well, he hung his head a bit, disappointed-like, and muttered 'OK, I'm sorry.' and walked away. Jackie, the breath got caught in my throat. I opened my mouth to call him, but nothing came out. In my mind I saw myself running after him, but in reality I couldn't move my feet, couldn't budge a single inch. I was paralyzed."

"Can you remember how you felt at that point?" Jackie asked.

Without skipping a beat, Sandra said "I felt like I

had failed him... like I had somehow wronged him. I only saw the man maybe twice a year and it had been over a year at that time. It's not fair..." Sandra's voice trailed off.

"What's not fair?" asked Jackie.

"Something else gripped hold of me at that very moment. Guilt. It gripped me hard. And I've been carrying it around ever since. And I'm tiiiiiiiiiiired! It's just not fair. *I* was the child! *HE* was the adult! Why am I carrying around this guilt? Why couldn't he forgive me?"

Jackie held off on any more questions. She sat in silence and handed Sandra a box of tissues so she could tend to her tears. Sandra felt awkward crying publicly about this. The incident with her dad taught Sandra that some tears in life should be reserved and shed in private. This incident also marked the moment that the devil taught her to suffer in silence... alone. (That's how his seeds take root and grow, you know? In silence... alone.) Sandra went home that night after the encounter with her dad in silence. She was a quiet child, so her mom didn't make a big deal of her lack of conversation. She made it through dinner, and retreated to her room. She crumbled up in bed and cried her heart out until she fell asleep. Sandra swore that when her father came back to clear up what happened, she would run to him and jump in his arms - like she couldn't before - and apologize for not recognizing him. She imagined herself begging for forgiveness, and him holding her and telling her it was alright... that he understood... that she was forgiven. But, that didn't happen. Because he never came back. Never. That's how bad she had hurt him. That's how bad his heart had been broken. And over time, she convinced herself that she simply did not deserve his love. She had wronged him, and possibly embarrassed him, in her inability to recognize and acknowledge him as the one who gave her life.

Over the next few weeks Jackie and Sandra worked through her feelings about her father. The incident emerged as the root of many of the issues Sandra dealt with during her adolescent years. The guilt she had about rejecting her father manifested in her rejection of love and affection from other men as well. She suffered from low self-esteem, considering herself unworthy of love, causing her to reject every romantic advance made towards her. She didn't know how to receive compliments and acknowledgements and therefore didn't have any sense of self-worth. She let down her guard a bit in high school, when she started to form what would turn out to be her lifelong friendships. But she was still very guarded, very protective of that bitter root of guilt. On some unconscious level, she didn't even think she deserved to be free of it... She didn't think she deserved the love of *any* man.

All of this meant disaster for Sandra's relationships. By the age of 28, although she had finally been on a few dates (just a few), and had had sex with plenty of men, she had never given any man her whole heart. They could have her time, her money, her body, and even a listening ear when they were in distress. But, her heart? Never! Nope! So she had never had a true boyfriend. That's not the saddest part though. The saddest part is that although she had been living a saved lifestyle for the past 7 years, worshipping God, and seeking to serve Him, that guilt was stopping her from accepting God's love. She could accept His deliverance, His healing, His assignment for her life. But she was incapable of accepting His love. She projected her perceptions of how her earthly father must've felt about her onto her heavenly Father. So, every time she felt some twinge of conviction for doing something she probably shouldn't be doing, in her mind that translated into God being severely angry with her. When she would hear God in her prayer time start to dote over her and speak kind words to her, in her mind this translated into God trying to manipulate her. In her mind, the only possible reactions God could have toward her were those that she felt her physical father must have had. Anger. Disappointment. Hurt. Disdain. She didn't understand the love of a natural father, so how could she ever understand the love of a heavenly Father?

Part 3

Jackie did her best over the next few months to help Sandra sort through her feelings regarding her father, and men in general. It was no small task, but Jackie felt they were making great progress in terms of helping Sandra not project her daddy issues onto the men in her life. Then one day, as they closed out their session, Jackie asked Sandra a question.

"Have you ever considered seeking pastoral counseling regarding your feelings towards God? Your inability to accept fully that he loves you?"

Pastoral counseling? Sandra had never considered any other type of counseling aside from what she was meeting Jackie once each week for. "Pastoral counseling?"

"Yes" replied Jackie. "It might be helpful."

"Are you trying to get rid of me?" Sandra joked.

"Not at all." Jackie said with a smile. "But I do think that someone more knowledgeable about your particular faith would be better qualified to help you with this part of your journey. You wouldn't have to sign up for ongoing sessions, necessarily. But you might be able to get some insight out of a few conversations that could help break down this guilt making your faith journey as rich as possible." Jackie paused. "Sandra, you once shared with me that you began this journey with me because you wanted to get all that God had for you out of this life. You wanted His plans for your success to be made manifest in your life, and you knew you had to get past the incident in order to really work towards this life in God. Well, I may not know very much about Christianity. But I do know that loving God and loving each other is a huge part of it. It would be a shame if you missed out on this part of your faith journey simply because you couldn't come to an understanding of the love of God."

Sandra nodded her head in agreement. She was happy that she was finally working through her issues with love and men. And Jackie was right. How could she fully serve a God that she didn't believe loved her? Why would she *want* to serve a God that she didn't believe loved her? Sandra said "I don't know where to get any pastoral counseling. I don't think my pastor offers it. And I'm not sure if I'd want to go to him with this anyway. Too close to home, you know?"

Jackie smiled and said "Yes, I understand." Then she flipped through the pages of her day organizer, looking for something. She stopped on a page and pointed to a number. "If you'd like, I can recommend someone. I have a colleague, an old classmate of mine, who is a licensed therapist. But he is also a minister, and specializes in Christian counseling at his church. Do you think you might like his information, in case you decide to give it a try? He's good at what he does, and I trust him." Sandra agreed to take the information, but she made no promises that she would call. She held on to his contact information and told Jackie she would let her know if she decided to pursue it.

Part 4

Minister Jason Simmons ran bible study at his church every Tuesday night. On this particular Tuesday, several weeks after Jackie had shared his information with Sandra, he had planned to teach about grace. Sandra walked in and took a seat, nodding her head and smiling at a few people as she did so. She had called that previous Friday to inquire about his pastoral counseling services. She was ready to tackle her "love of God" issues, but said she'd like to come to an actual service before making an appointment to be seen one-on-one. This wasn't foreign to Jason. Many Christians didn't want to sit in on a counseling session with him until they heard him teach or preach the word of God. This was their litmus test as to whether or not he could be "trusted". If he could preach or teach the Word of God effectively, then he could be trusted to counsel them. If not, they'd politely decline, although no one had done so yet. Jason approached Sandra's unfamiliar face and extended his hand. "Hello, I'm Minister Jason. Welcome to New Hope Tabernacle."

Sandra accepted his hand and said, "Hello Minister Jason. I'm Sandra. We spoke on the phone last week."

"I thought you might be Sandra!" he smiled broadly. "It's good to meet you."

"Likewise," said Sandra, "Thank you."

"Sister Sandra, we're going to get started in just a few minutes. Did you have any questions before

Praise and Worship begins?"

"No, I'm just hoping that God speaks to me tonight. I feel like I need to hear from Him in the worst way."

"Well that'll be my prayer for you tonight. So sit back and enjoy. Feel free to worship with us and participate however you feel led."

"Thank you so much." said Sandra. In that moment, the praise team made their way out to the stage. The musicians began to play and the praise leaders asked the congregation to stand on their feet. Sandra obliged. They sang a few contemporary Christian songs she was familiar with. She felt at home. She knew God was indeed there. And the people were kind. They were true worshippers. Then, the praise team began a song she was unfamiliar with. She remained standing, of course, and tried to get into the flow of it. But honestly, she was just so annoyed with the lead singer. She was repeating the refrain of the song over and over and over again… for way too many times. It looked like she was feeling something while leading this particular song, as she was bent over in a worship position, with her eyes closed, singing intently. But Sandra was just wishing they would move on to another song already. She kept glancing at her reflection in the plexiglass that encased the drummer to make sure her face didn't indicate how annoyed she was.

After about 5 minutes of the same refrain over and over, Sandra sat down. She couldn't get with the program. She was almost ready to leave. But she clearly heard the voice of God say "Wait. Listen". She heard His voice so clearly she had no choice but to be obedient. So she quieted down. And listened. The worship leader continued to sing the same refrain. The words were *"Your love never fails, never gives up, never runs out on me."* She sang these words over and over and over. Sandra thought to herself "Ok, Lord, here goes this issue of love again... but what are you saying to me???" As the song continued to be sung, now in greater volume as the congregation had joined in, He brought the incident to Sandra's remembrance again. The pain resurfaced, although not as sharply as it was just a few months prior. But God, again, began to clearly, yet gently speak.

"Sandra, your earthly father REALLY and TRULY did love you. But he couldn't handle what he assumed was your rejection of him. So even with the abundance of love he had for you, it wasn't enough to overcome the pain he felt. Sometimes, the greater you love someone, the greater capacity you have to get hurt by them." Tears began to fall from Sandra's eyes. She heard God clearly. And she understood everything He was saying. She could still hear the refrain being sung in the background.

Your love never fails, never gives up, never runs out on me...

"Lord, I just wish I had a chance to explain to him what happened. It's not fair!" Sandra screamed internally. "I just wanted a chance to explain. He'll never know how sorry I was... how sorry I am." A few moments passed before Sandra got a response. She heard, "If your father were right here, right now, what would you say to him?" Suddenly, Sandra felt a cool breeze. She tightened her eyes as the wind blew and caused some tears that had pooled into the corners of her eyes to fall. She shuddered a bit, then opened her eyes. Right there in the middle of the worship service, Sandra had what some would describe as an open vision. She was back in that afterschool classroom again. She was sitting at a desk, the same desk she remembered herself standing behind when *the incident* happened. She was of course bigger in this space now, so it seemed to consume her a bit. Her legs didn't fit under the desk unless she stretched them out. Sandra began to take in her surroundings unable to believe what she was seeing. She looked around the room. The sun shone brightly through the windows. There were brightly colored drawings hanging on the walls. It looked like students had yet to visit the space that day. Everything was tucked away in its place, nice and neat. There was no one else around. There was a calm in the air. She felt none of the anxiety usually associated with remembering that space and time – until she heard the voice. "Excuse me", the voice spoke from the door. Sandra looked up and when she did, her heart sank into her belly. "Hi little girl", the man said with a smile.

"Daddy?" The word barely escaped Sandra's mouth. She could not believe she was looking into the face of her father.

"Come on and give me that hug you've been wanting! I've been waiting for it too!"

Sandra got weak in the knees. She tried to stand up in excitement and ended up falling back into the seat. Her father chuckled and said "Awwww, come on. You're way too young to be struggling to stand up." At that comment, Sandra wondered if he saw her as she truly was. Then she wondered if she was really seeing what she thought she was seeing. But she shook these thoughts out of her head. This was her moment. This was what she'd been waiting for for almost 30 years. She stood up, more steadily this time, and ran over to her father. She stopped right at the threshold, and he opened his arms to welcome her in. She allowed her face to fall into his chest as she wrapped her arms around his midsection. He then wrapped his arms around her. Sandra began to sob violently.

"I missed you." her father said.

"I missed you too" Sandra replied, though muffled by his chest. They rocked from side to side as they embraced. She took in his scent. He smelled familiar. He smelled good. He was nice and warm too, a little pudgy, which felt nice.

After a few moments, her father loosened his embrace and said "Let me look into that face." He gently held Sandra by the shoulders and pushed her slightly back. He gazed at her lovingly. Sandra didn't know how to respond. "Little girl, you are

GORGEOUS. I don't think I ever made nothing quite as wonderful as you."

"Really Daddy?" Sandra asked incredulously through tears.

"O' course! You were my late in life child. You was always special to me." The tears began to fall heavily again from Sandra's eyes. She wanted to hear her father talk all day, every day. His country twang was so endearing. "What's all this crying about Little girl?" her father inquired.

Sandra was busting at the seams with remorse. She exclaimed "I'M SOOOOO SORRY DADDY!"

"Sorry? For what, now? What'chu talkin' bout?" He gripped her shoulders a bit firmer and stared into her face.

"Daddy I'm sorry I said I didn't know you that day. I realized right away that I was wrong, but I just didn't recognize you. And I've wanted to apologize all these years for hurting you. But you never came back. And when you never came back, I knew I musta hurt you real bad, Daddy. I am SO SORRY. PLEEEASE forgive me." Sandra heard the words spill from her mouth like a faucet. It was like a cleansing of sorts… a soul cleansing.

"Aww Sandra, I wasn't mad at you! You don't have nothing t' apologize for."

"I don't?" Sandra asked.

"Naaawww" Her father reassured her. She looked up into his face and he was smiling so brightly. "When you said you didn't know me, Sandra. Yes, I was disappointed. But I was disappointed with myself."

"Why, what do you mean Daddy?"

"See, that day, I realized that my less-than-occasional dropping by had caused my own child to not know me. I saw your face Little girl. I saw you tryna figure out where you knew me from. And you honestly had NO idea. That had me to feel like the biggest loser of a father in the world."

Sandra listened intently to this explanation her father was giving. Was he saying he didn't blame her for their separation? "But Daddy, I saw it. I saw the look in your face when I said I didn't know you. I saw your heart break. I know I did Daddy!"

"Yea, Little girl. My heart did break. My heart broke knowing that my daughter didn't know me, and it was all my fault. My heart broke knowing that if I said 'Yea, you know me. I'm your daddy!' that teacher woulda looked at me like the piece of crap I felt like. She would have known that I was a deadbeat whose child didn't even recognize him. And she woulda been right. I wasn't mad at you, Sandra. I was mad at myself… and ashamed."

Sandra didn't know how to respond. She stood with her mouth open, dumbfounded. She was trying to sort through her emotions and come up with something to say, but she couldn't seem to formulate any words. Her father saw the look on her face, and he held up his hand as if to say "stop". "Sandra, last time, you *couldn't* say anything. This time, you don't *have to* say anything. You don't owe *me* an apology. I owe *you* an apology. I am sorry I had you to carry around all that guilt. My pride was bruised that day. You held a mirror up to me and I didn't like the reflection I saw. I realized how little I contributed to your life. And I figured you'd be better off without me coming around. No more once in a while phone calls. No more occasional drop-bys. No more confusion. So when I saw that you honestly just could *NOT* remember me, I decided it might be best if you never had to worry about me ever again. I honestly thought that was the best thing to do."

Sandra felt a surge of... rage, was it? Whatever it was, it wasn't the remorse she started out with. "So you said NOTHING, Daddy?!?!"

"Can you forgive me, Sandra?"

Whoa, whoa, whoa!, Sandra thought to herself. This was too much. Not only was she supposed to accept that he chose his pride over his daughter, she was supposed to forgive him? Sandra began to feel her ego puff up. But before it had a chance to get too full, she heard a voice behind her. "Sandra!" She knew that voice. It was God speaking. Sandra turned around to see no one there. The only thing moving was the sunlight streaming through the window. She watched it dance and said "Yes, Lord?"

"Didn't you want your father to forgive you when you thought you had hurt him?"

"Yes. That's all I wanted. That's all I ever wanted."

"Well what if he wanted your forgiveness? What if pride led to a foolish decision on his part, and he came back wanting your forgiveness? Would you give it to him?"

"But that's not fair!" Sandra exclaimed. "I've been hurting all these years! And now he comes and tells me it actually wasn't my fault? And I'm supposed to forgive him?! *He* was the adult! *He* should have handled it better than that!"

"Better than how you're handling this now?"

Sandra stood in confused silence. Her tantrum went from a level 5 to a level 2. "What?"

"I asked you what you would say to your father if you had the chance. You used this opportunity to ask him to forgive you for some wrong you thought you had done to break his heart. Now, he stands before you asking you to forgive him for a wrong he did that broke your heart. Will you extend the same forgiveness to him that you yourself wanted?" Sandra was stunned. She had no response. She could feel her heart beating steadily in her chest. This was supposed to be *her* moment. This was supposed to be *her* time to cleanse herself, to purge all guilt. What was happening? Had God led her into some crazy trap? "Sandra, he won't be at the door very long. This time, he MUST go. He cannot stay here while you figure it out. Look at him Sandra."

Sandra turned back to her father. He patiently waited on her response. He looked tormented. Utterly tormented. And guilt-ridden. The face that a few moments ago smiled so brightly was now haggard with worry, regret, and anxiety. He looked how she felt... all 30 years of it. "No one should have to carry those feelings." This came from yet another voice. It was a child's voice. Sandra spun around to see herself as a child, once again standing behind that desk.

"What did you say?" asked Sandra.

"No one should have to carry those feelings" said the smaller version of herself. Sandra looked at her and her heart welled up with sorrow again. She was right. She knew first-hand that no one should have to carry around such overwhelming feelings of guilt and regret. Sandra turned back to look at her father. A few moments passed by without either of them saying anything. Then, he hung his head a bit, disappointed-like, and muttered 'OK, I'm sorry.' and he turned to walk away... again. Sandra's breath got caught in her throat. She opened her mouth to call him, but nothing came out. Suddenly something penetrated the air. "DAAADDDYYYYYYYY!" Little Sandra screamed at the top of her lungs with pure uninhibited desperation in her voice. She ran past Sandra, crossing the threshold to her father in the hallway. He turned around, and Little Sandra jumped in his arms and cried, "Yes, I forgive you Daddy! I forgive you! And I love you! And I understand!"

Lee held little Sandra tightly. He squeezed her and rocked her and cried as he kissed her all over her face. This was what love looked like - forgiveness.

Sandra again began to cry. She wanted in on the love fest that was erupting in the hallway. She needed it. She began to cross the threshold to reach out to her Dad. She held her hand out for him to grab. He looked her intently in the eyes. He released one arm from around little Sandra, still holding her firmly with the other, and extended his free arm out towards Sandra. As she walked into the hallway, she began to say, as she looked up into her father's face, "I love you Daddy. I love you Daddy. I love you Daddy." over and over again. But before she could really embrace him, her open vision ended, and she was back in the sanctuary at New Hope Tabernacle, with her hand outstretched, looking up towards the sky, saying "I love you Daddy, I love you Daddy, I love you Daddy" over and over again. Then God said, "I love you too. I always have. And I always will. No matter what." She heard God clearly. And she understood everything He was saying. And she could hear the refrain still being sung in the background.
Your love never fails, never gives up, never runs out on me…

"Sandra, your father walked away from the door. That was his choice. You were not to blame. But, know this: I will NEVER respond by walking away from the door. Instead, I will CONTINUE to stand at the door. I will CONTINUE to wait for you to acknowledge Me, for you to recognize me. Because I love you THAT MUCH." As God spoke, Sandra felt a flood of emotion overcome her body. She couldn't stand under it, and ended up crumpled up in a ball on the floor. Then, she felt a warmth come over her body. It was kind of like the warmth of her father's hug in her vision, but more intense. It was like the blanket she draped over herself during her morning devotions, but heavier. Safer. She heard God clearly. And she understood everything He was saying. And she could still hear the refrain being sung in the background.

Your love never fails, never gives up, never runs out on me…

Part 5

The crowd that gathered at New Hope Tabernacle never made it past Praise and Worship that night. The presence of God was so heavy, and so powerful, that they didn't get to the actual bible study lesson about grace. But God had given Sandra her own personal lesson on the topic. That night, the crowd that had assembled sang songs to God all night, basking in His love for them. Sandra got a revelation of God's love that was even more profound than she thought it could be. She was by no means suddenly 100% guilt free. But she had received directly from God the assurance that he would love her unconditionally. She could not have asked for a greater ending to her night.

The next morning, when Sandra woke up, she did her usual mirror routine. She checked her face, slightly less critically than usual. Then she looked into her eyes, and she smiled. She grabbed her blanket and Bible and headed towards her living room chair for devotion time. This time, she started out by getting on her knees to pray.

> *"Daddy, God. Thank you. My heart is overwhelmed by the love I felt last night. I am still speechless. I heard You loud and clear. I know Your love will never fail like man's sometimes fails. And I know that my greatest expression of love can be to forgive, and love anyway, even when I feel I have been wronged. I pray that my trust in You will grow. I pray that I never forget the words You spoke to me. I've written them down and I'll mediate on them every time I start to feel far from You. Continue to work on me, Lord. I want You to continue healing my heart. Now Lord, as I begin to search Your Word, direct me to where You want me to reflect this morning. Show me Your heart towards me, yet again, this morning. I say this prayer in Jesus' name. Amen."*

Sandra got up off her knees, sat in her chair, wrapped the blanket around her arms, and began to flip through the pages of her Bible. She landed in the book of Deuteronomy, chapter 31. She began to read, and stopped in awe and smiled when she got to verse 8, which states "The Lord himself goes before you and will be with you; he will never leave you nor forsake you. Do not be afraid; do not be discouraged." (Deuteronomy 31:8, NIV). She heard God clearly. And she understood everything He was saying. And she could still hear the refrain being sung in the background.

Your love never fails, never gives up, never runs out on me…

HEARTBREAK

"This is the last time"
I said this then I looked in your face.
You were in mid-stroke.
I'll never forget that moment as I watched your whole demeanor change.
For a moment I felt
Omniscient
Omnipotent
because as I looked into your eyes I saw your spirit split in two.
And I KNEW it was me that did it.

"That's heartbreak" I said to myself.
I had never broken anyone's heart before.
Strangely, I then felt accomplished.
It was perverse.

I suppose it's because I had been so

distrusting of them (men)
including you (especially you),
that I never really believed
that any one of you had ever really loved me.
As far as I had been concerned
It was all just game.
Well-rehearsed,
convincingly acted out
Game.
I never thought twice about ending any relationship.
It came so easy.
When I had finally successfully convinced myself that
I was being played,
I simply stopped answering the phone.
I ended the infatuation as quickly as it began.
Every shred of care or concern was either buried deep somewhere in my subconscious or tossed out like last week's leftovers (no longer appetizing, nor satisfying).

I didn't give a fuck.

I
Didn't.
Give.
A FUCK.

You aint gonna play me!

But then, as I stood there
looking into your eyes,

not only did I feel something,
I felt a lot of
somethings.
The emotions were overwhelming.
Sadness…
because I had selfishly taken away the last person that
showed any real concern for you and your well-being.
Satisfaction…
because I had finally made you and
(as far as I was concerned)
every
other
man
that had ever paid me insecurities
and earned my doubt,
CRUMBLE
with one simple statement.
"This is the last time."

THE RELEASE

My friendships are changing. And that's gonna have to be alright with me. In my mind, I tried to hold on too long. But the truth of the matter is, if I release you in my mind, the way I've released you physically, it'll free up some of my energy. Thus, allowing you to do you, and allowing me to do me. It's not about goodbye. Because I know if you called me tomorrow I'd be there. But when you don't call, or when I don't call, because we know there's really nothing to talk about, there won't be any more guilt about it. I have to be alright with this. It's like Jesus approached me on my boat and said "follow me and I'll make you a fisher of men". I have yet to drop my net, although my heart is with Him. I can't bring myself to drop my net. You've been my net, my safety net, and it's just so hard to let go. You're what I'm used to. You're what I've always relied on. You're a certainty in my life when everything He offers just seems so uncertain.

I keep looking back at what we had. Our walk together was beautiful... was necessary. But it was an old path. I've been given my new marching orders and have been afraid to carry them out. Not because I'm afraid of your opinion of my new path. I've passed that phase. But, because I've never done anything new without you. You've been here throughout so many years. All my starts and stops. And I know this new start will not be shared with you. That scares me. It saddens me. I want my friends by my side when I do this. But it is not to be. Not right now. This is my walk. My path. And I can't expect you to walk it with me. We've taken a mighty long walk together already. It was beautiful. But it's counterproductive for me to wait for you to fall in step with me. So I'll walk. I'll walk on. Knowing that I'll never walk alone. Because "Oh, what a friend I have in Jesus."
He walks with me.
He talks with me.
He tells me that I am His own.
That's what the songs say anyway.
I guess it's time to try Him for myself.

LET THE WALL COME DOWN

I've been re-examining my relationships lately... all of them. And realize I need to step up my game in terms of showing the people I REALLY care about that they are important to me. My desire to stay drama-free has led me to disassociate with too many people I love. I said I stayed away because their unrighteous behavior was something I couldn't deal with. But, the reality is, if I'm honest, I just didn't want to slip back into my ways. Didn't want to be tempted by the lusts of the world.

The reality is, I thought their unrighteousness would somehow make me unrighteous. And I chose not to love them enough to deal with that.

I also shy away from engaging with my saved friends with the worry – if I'm honest – that the "real" me would seep through. I've been guarded and hiding behind a wall my entire Christian walk. Not wanting to go back to the old me, and not wanting anyone to see that I'm not perfect. But I'm tired of doing that. It has profited me NOTHING. And it has been a miserable experience.

The people I care about don't really know ME. They only know the parts of me I allow to be seen. I hide a LOT of my real self, as if that somehow protects me from rejection…
somehow makes me more holy…
somehow keeps me saved.
But it doesn't.
It's only resulted in my not knowing how to fully function and SHOW UP in the real world… not knowing how to interact with my family and friends.

I'm ready to really live. To really experience life. I'm ready. I need God to equip me now. Because I'm ready. I'm ready to be me. I've been walking with others, but essentially alone, for a long time *only* because I refused to TRULY partner with those around me. I didn't want them to see the ugly me. People see my light so easily. I didn't want to diminish God's glory by portraying anything less than an image of perfection. In reality, the level of glory they see is no comparison to the glory that would be revealed if I was being the real me. In my weakness, His strength can be seen. Why kill myself trying to be strong when if I'm just me, his strength will show up? I'm ready to stop being so guarded. I'm ready to let the wall come down.

I'M SORRY

I'm sorry if I don't wear enough make-up for you.
But see when I get down on my knees to pray
or stand up on my feet to praise,
I don't need to be worried about my eyeliner or mascara running down my face.
Can't be hindered by Revlon or Cover Girl
Because God said I'm already his "cover girl".
I am fearfully and wonderfully made.
I am the apple of His eye.
He makes His face to shine upon me
And so,
No,
I need no foundation to cover my marks.
He *is* my foundation.
He's already covered my marks,
Erased my sins,
Cast them in the sea of forgetfulness.
He's lined my lips
With his words,

Pierced my ears with them too
This is what makes effective the message I deliver to you.
To see clearly in the Spirit,
I don't need them any curlier or longer – *my eyelashes*.
Because He said He'd give me beauty for something even stronger – *my ashes*.
So when I take off Sundays best and throw on sackcloth,
Mind me NOT!
It means I'm in a state of supplication,
Shamelessly crying out for restoration,
And I simply cannot afford (nor do I have the time) to "blush".
But that's alright, because
When Mac runs out and Sephora shuts down
He'll always have a way to make me blush.
So, I'm sorry…

I'm sorry if I'm not more quiet in prayer…
That I sometimes draw attention,
Run around,
Talk in tongues.
But like I said earlier, I am God's cover girl
So when he puts a nation before me in the Spirit
He's saying "cover it girl!"
Like Rizpah.
I can't care if there are vultures overhead,
Or if I don't eat,
Or if I lose sleep,
Or sometimes never even make it to bed!

Or if you think I'm crazy!
Because sometimes,
This is what it takes to appeal to the King.
And like Esther, this may be my only chance.
Positioned as Plain Jane, but with obvious potential.
Let the King, not this world, mold me
So I will be fit to present my petitions before Him.
And in doing so,
Sometimes I need to wail, I need to moan, and can't be concerned with who hears it!
So, I'm sorry if I'm not more quiet.
He called for the weeping women
To come beat their breasts
And I can't afford to fail that test.
So excuse me if I cry louder,
And LOUDER,
Especially if at that time I'm receiving POWER!
Yes, I can be noisy.
But please believe me, I'm still a lady.
A wife, to be exact.
His bride to be.
So in my preparation there's excitement.
YOU should be excited too!
He's getting me ready,
And he's getting me ready JUST FOR YOU!
So forgive me!
Forgive me if I walk up and down the aisles as I shout.
I know you'd prefer some quiet "halleluiahs".
But he said let EVERYTHING that hath breath praise the Lord.

SO, I'm praising him in anticipation,
In expectation,
In spite of the hardship,
In lieu of the breakthrough.
And you know what?
Sometimes,
I'm even praising him for you.
So, I'm sorry boo
If you think I'm not the girl for you.

I'm sorry.

I'm sorry if my hair is not more stylish.
No color
No bangs
No wigs
No tracks
Not a curl or a wave.
Just plain
Pushed back
Or straight down
And most of the time covered by scarf or hat.
But see, I was told that my hair is my glory.
And with you as my "head"
All this glory is reserved for you.
For YOU!
So we
Can give it to HIM!
From us to Him.
Don't need other men staring at it,
lusting over it - *as you know yall do.*

So for now,
I'll preserve it.
You deserve it!
I'll keep it covered just for you.
And for Him too.
'Cuz, you see, I was told that this is how I should approach my king
At His throne,
Head covered in prayer.
And I can't be worried that my cherry coke rinse might stain my prayer shawl
When I approach the altar to give him my all.
So at this phase in my life, the dip do will have to wait.

Speaking of weight,
I'm sorry.

I'm sorry I'm not more petite in my frame.
My shoulders are broad and my back is not the straightest.
But whether you approve or not,
this is what helps me carry the burden for the nations,
In my belly.
So see
I can't help my frame.
And you know what else?
I can't help my name!
It was given to me.
I'm sorry it's not more regular.

Less different.
But when you hear the name Inacent
It should speak volumes.
I should speak volumes.
My mother named me for a play character that was a prophet.
My heavenly Father formed me before my mother was thought of, as a prophet.
So my mother simply spoke
something that wasn't
as if it was
and it became
and so my name
is
perfect!
I AM PERFECT,
For right now.
And striving everyday to become more like Him every day.
And I'm convinced
That one day soon, He will present me.
My Father will present me.
And when he does, it will be the presentation fit for the Daughter of a King.
Better than any Bat Mitzvah
Quinceañera
Sweet 16
Cotillion
Coming out Ceremony
Or Rites of Passage.
And the gifts

In my possession,
Will bring me before great men.
Regardless of a manicure or pedicure
He'll still get glory from the works of my hands
And the scars on my feet
Because as the poet once said, "Scarred are the feet that follow He!"
And me?
Oh My!
I just can't wait for that time.
But in the meantime…

I'm sorry.

Sorry I'm not playful and flirtatious.
Sorry I won't smile in your face
and bat my eyes
just to try and make you smile.
Like I said, he's exchanging my beauty for ashes,
so when you see me repenting,
When you see me fasting,
When you see me travailing in prayer,
That ALONE should make you smile.
Because the truth is, them flirtatious, smile-in-your face women won't come near to balancing your power.
Those silly giggly women couldn't pray you out of a brown paper bag.
They'll be busy looking into your eyes
When they should be looking into the Spirit.
Your true heart is in the Spirit.

I will look for you in the Spirit.
And hope you meet me.
I AM your help meet.
So when our souls meet,
If you're not satisfied with my physicality
and you still don't want me,
Then – most of all –
For YOU…
I
am
SORRY!

I WAS BORN TO SERVE YOU

I never understood what it meant for wives to be submitted.
I never understood what it meant to be a help meet.
I never really cared.
We're not even married... not even courting...
But something in me wants to submit to you.
Wants to help you.
Wants to complete you.
I see the areas I can complement you in and it excites me.
It draws me.
It motivates me.
I want to get down to work.
I want to be productive with you.
I want to till with you.
I want to plant with you.
I want to cultivate with you.
I want to fill the gaps.

I want to handle the things you don't think of but I know are necessary.
I want to do it without your asking me to.
I want to do it without asking your permission to.
But our relationship is not such right now that my autonomy to operate concerning the affairs of your life would be appropriate.

I want to do your behind the scenes work.
I want to be the producer of your stage-play.
I want to be your stage hand… your set designer.
I don't need a starring role.
I don't want to be center stage when the curtain rises.
I want to stand backstage and watch as you take your bow.
I want to make things happen for you.
I want to make it happen.
I want to make you happy.
I want you to be pleased.
I want to hear you say "well done".
It matters when you say "well done".
If no one else likes it, as long as you and God like it, then my assignment is complete.
Am I talking recklessly?
Well, that's how I feel.
I can get 1,000 compliments from 1,000 people and it would mean nothing
if you did not give your approval.

I trust you.
I trust your leadership.

I trust your ability to lead and your vision.
I respect you.
I respect your vision.
I see your vision.
I inherently carry your vision.
I want to give birth to it.
I'm brought to travail over it.
I feel the moanings and groanings of it within me.
I want to push it out.
I'm ready to push.
I'm ready to bear down and bring into existence what you have conceived.
I'm ready for the pain, the tears, the sweat, the blood.
The Blood,
It covers us.
I feel closer knitted to Christ up under your covering.
You are my perfectly made covering.
I nest in you.
I don't know if you know it.
Do you know it?
Do I feel like a good fit for you?
I think you know it.
I pray you know it.
I sense you know it.
But you have not budged.
Not in the natural.
I know you're planning... almost plotting.
That word sounds so devious, but it's appropriate.
It's a plot between you and Daddy.
To be carefully executed.
How important am I to be the subject of such a

mighty plot?
How precious am I to be pursued with such intention that neither you nor Daddy feels you can afford to mess this up?
Can't move too soon.
But you can't wait too long either.

Your existence makes the Song of Solomon make sense.
Long misunderstood,
This Song of Songs speaks to me now.
I understand it now.
He said…
 As an apple tree among the trees of the forest,
   so is my beloved among the young men.
With great delight I sat in his shadow,
   and his fruit was sweet to my taste.
He brought me to the banqueting house,
   and his banner over me was love.
Sustain me with raisins;
   refresh me with apples,
   for I am sick with love.
His left hand is under my head,
   and his right hand embraces me!
I adjure you, O daughters of Jerusalem,
   by the gazelles or the does of the field,
that you not stir up or awaken love
   until it pleases
(Song of Solomon 2:3-7, ESV)

You are an apple tree, good for refreshing in a forest

of other less useful trees.
Less useful to me, anyway.
They're good for shade.
Some women only require shade.
Any random stump will due as long as they can be propped up and cooled down.
But I need more.
I require the nourishment, the refreshing, the sweetness that no other tree in this forest provides.
I used to question myself.
My refusal to sit under other trees.
Surely there's nothing wrong with shade.
They weren't bad trees.
But I wanted more.
I needed more.
I need a tree with fruit.
I sit under your shade with GREAT delight.
Your fruit, your teaching, your impartation… *is* sweet and pleasing and satisfying to my palette.
This is what I've wanted.
You accepted me into your banquet house, where I have been shown true love.
You have sustained the portion of me that was previously established with nuggets that reinforce who I am.
You renew me with your fruit.
Your left hand is under my head as you impart wisdom that blows my mind.
Your right hand of embrace is your covering and protection as you do so.
This love is real.

This is the love they refer to when they speak of "true" love.
There's nothing false or fake about it.
This love is not an emotion.
I can't even identify the emotions that accompany this love.
This love... absolutely should not be awakened, nor stirred up, before it pleases.
I understand Solomon.
Whether his song be interpreted in the light of the Love of Christ or the love of you.
This love... absolutely should not be stirred up before it pleases.
But, it *is* stirred.
It *is* stirred
And it *is* stirring...
Steadily.
I cannot stop it.
I think it pleases.
The ladle circles the pot, even though I let it go.
This brew has a life of its own,
A mind of its own.
It pleases.

I wonder,
Do you know what this does to me?
Do you know what I'm feeling?
Can you discern my thoughts?
Do you even try?
Should you even try?
Do you *need* to try?

Or do I wear them on my sleeve?
Am I transparent in my attempts to be so guarded?
In a way, I hope so.
I want to be seen in my hiding.
I want to be understood in my hiding.
I want to be protected in my hiding,
In my waiting.
I am waiting.
I don't mind waiting.
My purpose is in the waiting.
I am learning in the waiting.
I'm learning what it means to be a help meet.
I'm learning what it means to be submitted.
I'm learning why
I was born to serve you.

MY FATHER'S FATHER

Today is my birthday.
I turned 23.
But it's also the birthday of my grandfather's
grandfather – before me.
So…
As my gift,
I do this for "we":
my grandfather's grandfather,
my grandfather's father,
my grandfather,
my father,
and me.

Our blood line is strong
and it runs real deep
deep…
deep…
deep down to the roots of the tree.
Blood soaked soil is where I plant my feet,

because battles were fought on this very ground
to make sure that I'd be free.
As a matter of fact my grandfather's grandfather swung from this tree,
was hung from this tree,
to make SURE I'd be free.
No matter where I go,
his spirit swings before me:
a spirit of what was
a spirit of what is
and a spirit of what is to be.
So you see,
It shouldn't surprise me that I'm swinging from the EXACT SAME TREE?

Well it's not the same tree.
The branches on my tree count 1… 2… 3.
Their system of checks and balances keeps the checks in their pockets and knocks me off balance every time.

They legally lynch me with their legislative branch.
The long arm of the law reaches out to me,
just to batter me.
The suits are not white robes and hoods,
but blue suits and hats,
and batons and bats,
that they crack like whips
on my head and my back.
These rats
come out

in the day and the night.
But this ain't a Cinderella story,
and they don't ride around on horses.
Their vehicles of choice have 1 motor, 4 wheels, and engines with the power of 1000 of horses,
with a "CPR" emblazoned on the side.
Courtesy… Professionalism… Respect...
Yeah, right!
I cracked your code mother fuckers,
and see that if you flip it,
CPR becomes RPC, or Regularly Pursuing Coons
Just like many, many moons
ago.
or flip it CPR: Constantly Pursuing Refugees
or flip it: Routinely Protecting Crackers
or flip it: Continuously Persecuting the Righteous
while Consistently Perpetuating Racism
by, flip it: Randomly Performing Checks
and flip it: Carelessly Popping Reckless shots!
And the blood at the roots just gets thicker.
So flip it!
Fuck it!
You got it,
Officer!
"But I'm innocent,
Your Honor!"

However,
that Judicial Branch always finds a way to justify the injustices I've suffered.
Mama sits in the courtroom,

hand over her mouth,
arm clutching her chest,
as she sees her only son being legally lynched.
I guess
she didn't think it could happen…
    again.
But why not?
After the Martins
Medgars
Malcolms
Mandellas
Mummias…
After the work of the national associations
rainbow coalitions
and action networks…
After the sit-ins
the marches
the rallies
the boycotts…
your boy still don't have that much of a shot
in the dark.
'Cuz in the dark,
they count mismarked ballots,
and miscount unmarked ballots.

The process they call an election
is more like a show by a magician.
While the commander and chief is flapping his lips and flailing his arms,
we don't see the bullshit he's dropping, or the harm it can cause.

See, I'm expertly executed by the executive branch.
Yes... a bird in the hand is worth 2 in the bush.
But are two Bushes in the white house worth my life
in the end?
I'm tired of it!
What am I to do?
What am I to think?
Who am I to be?
What about my seed?
My seed didn't ask for this tree.
Nor for this blood,
Nor for these roots,
but the truth
is that he'll inherit it.
He'll have to deal with it
the best way he can.
Like a strong, resilient, intelligent black man.

Can't you see?
If it don't stop now
he'll end up just like we,
hanging from this tree,
like my grandfather's grandfather,
my grandfather's father,
my grandfather,
my father,
and me.

FROM A DAUGHTER'S VACATION JOURNAL

While on a solo vacation in Puerto Rico in 2013 I encountered God at every turn. He spoke clearly and used every experience I had to illustrate something about my life. The following entry is a reprinting of a single day's worth of journal entries on a day I went to visit Castillo San Cristobal, the largest fort built by Spain in the New World. I stopped and wrote what He said after every encounter during this trip, including every stop I made while at the fort. I usually wouldn't share journal entries, but I hope something here will encourage or inspire someone else.

6/22/13

<u>Castillo San Cristobal</u>. It took 250 years to build this stronghold. And it was prompted by a series of attacks. It doesn't have to take forever for the Lord. The name of the Lord is already a strong tower. All

we have to do is run into it. Kingdom mindset is necessary. Military positioning is necessary. Know what weapons are at your disposal and use them. This fort still stands strong. Although a museum now, if a time of war were to come about it could still be used. In fact, I learned that it was put back into use as a base of operations during World War II in the 1940's.

Message: Don't let God become a museum. Don't let your strong tower only be used during times of war. During times of peace it's still necessary to know your way around... to maintain position.

While standing on a high point of the fort, He had me to look out at the beauty of His creation. We walked in the grass and He tickled my feet. I didn't care for the feel of the grass on my feet and so I tiptoed through it like the squeamish city girl that I am. He said I was a punk, how could a daughter of His be a punk? LOL But while looking out at the beauty of the mountains, the clouds, and the ocean, he reminded me that when I "hang out" with him I will see great things. He said there was not a part of this world I could not see if I wanted to. It's at my disposal and He'll always – ALWAYS – make a way. I cried right there. I saw Him (in the beauty of His creation). I smelt Him (the smell of the ocean). I felt Him (the grass on my feet). I heard him (His voice was very clear).

Another watchtower on the fort: When I entered into the watchtower, He said it was like my "secret place". So I began to pray aloud. The prayers echoed heavily off the walls. He said that's how it is in the secret place. Alone and shut off from the rest of the world, my prayers ECHO. He hears me that much louder, that more clearer, when I pray from my secret place. He told me to get comfortable in my secret place. Heaven hears me from there even the more.

Dinner With Daddy
I was invited to dinner with my Daddy tonight. I put on a dress, the only one I had with me. I wandered around Old San Juan for about 20 minutes until I happened upon an old Italian restaurant. I checked the menu outside and decided it tempted my palate. The young waiter escorted me up the steps and inside. There, the hostess greeted me and showed me to a table for two. I sat down and looked over the menu again. I couldn't decide. Daddy said "you can get whatever you want". I ordered a Caesar salad, a fishcake appetizer and a seafood linguine entree. I sat back and realized jazz was playing over the air. I smiled. The waiter came back and lit the candle on my table. I smiled again. I was about to have a feast – Father and daughter, King and princess. And it felt so right. I smiled again. Halfway through my salad, God spoke the most tender words a man has ever spoken to me. He said "Someday, he'll take you out to dinner like this. But I had to do it first. Someday, he'll take you on trips like this, but I had to do it

first." I fought back tears. I mean I really fought back tears. I'm sure my face was a contorted mess. I was filled with joy as I understood for the first time ever how precious I was to God, how much He loved me, how jealous He was over me. I was LOVED. Yes, it was a nice thought that I would one day take trips like this with a husband. But it was an even nicer though that my Father God in heaven wanted time like this alone with me. This trip is the most intimate I've ever been with God. Even in my most intense times of supplication, I've never felt this level of intimacy.

As I ate my appetizer, He said "let's talk". I waited for more of the dialogue it seemed we had been having thus far, but I heard nothing. So I opened the bible on my phone and remembered that last night I was going to be on my way to I Peter. So I went, expecting a word. And I got one. In chapter 1 it reads:

14 Like <u>children</u> ruled by God, do not go back to the old desires of the time when you were without knowledge:
15 But be holy in <u>every detail</u> of your lives, as he, whose servants you are, is holy;
16 Because it has been said in the Writings, You are to be holy, for I am holy.
17 <u>And if you give the name of Father to him</u> who, judging every man by his acts, has no respect for a man's position, <u>then go in fear while you are on this</u>

<u>earth</u>:
18 <u>Being **conscious** that you have been made free from that foolish way of life which was your heritage from your fathers</u>, not through a payment of things like silver or gold which come to destruction,
19 But <u>through holy blood</u>, like that of a clean and unmarked lamb, even the blood of Christ:
(I Peter 1:14-19, BBE)

This was my reminder from my Daddy, that now that I have been adopted as a Daughter, claim the title, and know in my heart of hearts that He *is* my Father, I ABSOLUTELY cannot turn myself back over to the old desires I once had. I have been living on the straight and narrow thus far. But this must mean that there must be some temptation coming that He feels the need to remind me of this. Also, since this scripture is also a call to holiness, perhaps He's trying to remind me of the absolute call to holiness over my life. I cannot waver from it. I can't let people or culture talk me out of it. I have to cling harder to it now in these days, especially in these days, as I move into ministry. As a child of God, a Daughter of a King, I can't go back to those old desires. I have to remain CONSCIOUS of the fact that through HOLY BLOOD, I have been made FREE from the FOOLISH way of life that was passed down to me from my bloodline, culture or society. I am now to live HOLY, as He who has made me free, and given me my NEW heritage, is HOLY. My NEW bloodline is a HOLY bloodline. So shall I be. AMEN.

IDENTITY CRY-SIS

Living in a world in which little girls are deciding that it's
too hard
To be a woman.
Or too degrading
Or too demanding
Or too victimizing
To be a woman.
It's too hard to be soft.
So hard that they're trying to
Walk like
Talk like
Fight like
Curse like
Be like
Be-come MEN.
And many boys
Are feeling like the pseudo-definition of masculinity and the low standard of manhood set for them by current pop culture is not one they feel comfortable

trying to stoop down to everyday.

Imagine,
His mother storms into the principal's office,
Tired of him getting bullied for his 12 inch weave, wrist flicking, and glitter lip gloss everyday
And says "I'd rather have my son be a well-mannered, respectable, young lady,
Than one of these
Pants sagging
Womanizing
Whoremongering
Weed smoking
Gang banging
Poor excuses for future men!"
Wow!
How emasculating
How feminizing
But she said it not realizing
The access she's given Satan
To rule over her son.
The power of life and death is in that tongue.
And those words,
breathed out of lips,
breeze past teeth,
and rush to open doors that welcome "the accuser" in.
Then we wonder why our children sin.
Whether it's the du-rag she's in
Or the pumps he walks in
The deceiver has successfully gained entrance.

And then…
He walks about like a lion,
seeking whom he may devour.
And young EVE looks up and sees the serpent
With so much going on around her,
And unsure of herself, her identity or her sexuality,
She is intrigued by a question:
"Why CAN'T I eat from this tree?"
Is she really forbidden?
But it looks just as good as the rest of God's fruit.
Even sweeter, because at least she does see a reflection of herself in it.
Have the Adams of this world moved so far away from the image of God that not only is it difficult to see God in him but it's difficult for Eve to see herself in him?
The rib can't see how she ever even came out of his cage…
So she's finding it hard to see herself going back in.

Meanwhile,
He's struggling within himself,
because the circumstances surrounding his health
are shaky… iffy.
If he
tests positive for HIV,
What will he do?
No, don't look at me that way.
I'm not one of those so-called Christians that thinks HIV is some punishment from God.
The God I serve is a good God.

And this dispensation of grace
Allows for some mistakes,
But Good GOD!
From the looks of the statistics, somebody's out to get our men
And since we know it's not God, who do YOU THINK it is then?
First no Eve, then no Eden
Hello Stephanie, Goodbye Steven!
The accuser strips him of every identifying mark.
So whether he's identifying as Mark
or identifying as Mary,
This situation is scary.
But the devil is a liar.
'Cuz there's still some GOD in Him.
The challenge is seeking to find it.
Christians get so caught up in appearances,
But we're supposed to be seeking to find it.
Christ is a redeemer of all things.
How dare you dismiss that sister or brother
as nothing more than a sinner,
Without taking just a little time, out of LOVE,
to stop and look on the inner?
Isn't that what Christ did for YOU?
Looked in on your inner-self,
Reached in and cleaned off your sinner's shelf,
And placed His heart on it?
So when u went out in the world
You could share His heart with every boy, with every girl?
We're taught to NOT be a respecter of persons.

But I hear the whispers:
"But he's carrying a purse!" and
"But she's walking with a bop!"
What's the use of whispering
If you're not even gonna stop
To say "hi", or "wasup" or
Share a bit of God with them?
How they gonna know Christ
if you don't show Him to them?
She might trade her bop for a bible,
And Him his purse for a cross.
But our HATRED turns them away,
That's why there are so many still lost.
So we should love the sinner,
And hate the sin,
And we can even hate the devil
That lured them in.
But that sister,
But that brother,
Deserve so much more
Than a church that's unwilling
To go to war for their souls!
Than a church that's unable to reflect the true glory of God,
Thru his grace, his mercy, and compassionate love.
Jesus said "Let he who is without sin cast the first stone."
First the elders, then the rest followed
Leaving God in his place on the throne!
For it is He that is the judge,
And He that is the Judge ALONE!

He doesn't need us to carry out his sentences.
But, by being Christ-like we can be his reflection
Of love
Of light
Of mercy
Of the life.
But instead,
WE'RE the ones with the identity Crisis,
Deciding if we will, or won't be
Like Christ.

IT'S NOT LOVE, IF IT'S HATE

Unless it's the love of God prompting you to hate sin, then it's not the righteousness of God. It's not the heart of God. You're being driven by pride, or hate, or rage, or jealousy. But it's not the Holy Ghost. If it were the Holy Ghost, although you'd despise the sin, you'd be driven to love the person. Don't think for a moment that those that gay-bash or bomb abortion clinics are doing the work of the Lord. He told us to love. And there are no ifs, ands or buts about it.

LOVE, LIKE, OR LUST
(PART 1)

Love, Like or Lust.
I can't figure it out.
I'm confused when I once wasn't.
I used to be sure.
Like the Song of Solomon asks
Are you a Wall or a Door?
And I was a WALL
Stood Strong and TALL.
Very Guarded.
And out of ALL
Of the women in my circle,
My friends and sisters,
I was the ONLY one not anxiously waiting for Boaz.
The only one not desperately seeking Stephen.
The only one not waiting to exhale or get my groove back.
I could care less.

I was content with my Word and my God and my prayer time.
But, back then,
When my mind would wander with thoughts of no-particular-him,
it was easier to distinguish a passing pleasant thought from a true aspiration of an "us" that I wanted to become.
And when my mind would wander to thoughts of bodies entangled in marriage-bed postures, but without the rings, my spirit would check my flesh,
I'd rebuke lust and cast it down, along with every thought that would exalt itself above the knowledge of what I KNOW to be God's true intentions for the exclusivity of my sexuality.
It was easier then.
Grace and Mercy kept me.
I had been freshly delivered from lust and all sexual immorality and was only thirsty for more of God, not more of any man.
And then, my admirers – they weren't so bold.
They did not pursue, because they knew I didn't play that!
They knew I was about my father's business.
I kid you not, I think I walked around with an impenetrable force field surrounding me that radiated Alpha and Omega Rays of Holiness, and with every step I took an angel would wag his finger at a would be admirer like "unh unh… not THIS one"
But now, it's different.
Now, I'm different.

Yes, now... 7 years later,
As I've allowed my Daddy to shape and mold me,
restore me and reform me,
redefine and refine me,
they've become very, very bold.
The smiles,
the unwelcomed - unsolicited chatter,
the relationship status inquiries,
the invitations for rides,
and dates,
and trips,
and Bible study...
Yes, Bible study!
My God!
I've never been invited to so many Bible studies,
and church programs,
and opportunities to collaborate,
and invitations to fellowship...
"Your place, or mine?
I mean your church, or mine?
I mean, why aren't you married yet?
I mean..."

Never before have I been so unsure about the reality or fallacy of my fantasies.
Who would have thought that becoming secure in my relationship with God
Would leave me open to being insecure and unsure about my relationships with men?
Whereas He once filled the void in my heart that I had evicted fornication, drugs, alcohol and partying

from,
A new void was forming.
I became curious about a mate.
And the church mothers don't make it no easier
"Chile, you done started preaching already. So where's your husband?"
And then they look at me like I'm doing something wrong!
And I wonder,
Am I doing something wrong?
Am I being too much of a wall?
Should I lower the force field?

And then,
It happened.
I met him.
I still don't know if he's THE him.
But he's "A" him.
A him that caught my eye,
My interest,
And maybe even my heart.
And suddenly,
The rules changed.
Whereas I previously didn't allow men to stay past 10 p.m. in my apartment,
I wanted him to stay as long as he pleased.
Where I typically fell asleep with a prayer shawl draping my shoulders,
Speaking into the ear of God,
I began staying up late on the phone with him –
His voice then become the one I needed to hear to

FROM PAIN TO PRAISE

ensure a good night's sleep.
And then,
Something happened…

                                          …to be continued

WILL YOU CARRY MY SON?

So, for the past 2 weeks I've been rolling a few things over in my mind about the Holiday season – Christmas specifically – Mary and Joseph, Jesus (of course), and I've been getting bits and pieces of clarity and revelation about several things. It all started when I heard a teaching by a great gift to the Body here in NY. He preached about imagining what it may have been like to be Mary and Joseph, with a heavy charge on our lives at such a young age to parent the Son of God. I'm sure many of us have heard preaching about this topic before. But for me, I heard it with new ears this time. He began to speak about what Mary must have felt like having an angel come to her and tell her that God wanted her to carry His Son. "I want you to carry My Son." The minister said it over and over. "I want you to carry My Son." And it began to occur to me that this message makes all of us like Mary in some way.

See, Mary was given the assignment to carry the actual body of the Son of God. I could imagine her being overwhelmed with such a charge and maybe even feeling a little unworthy. But it was definitely HER assignment. God said He wanted HER to carry His Son. Hasn't God asked us to do the same thing?

When we accept Christ as our Lord and Savior, we accept the assignment to "carry" Him inside of us. We are given the responsibility of "carrying" Jesus inside of us! Even further, as carriers of the Son of God we are expected to LET HIM LIVE, through us, as well! Just like Mary, we are asked to turn over our bodies so that Jesus may come forth in this world and live. This amazes me! We talk about the mystery of the immaculate conception, but if you're a born-again believer, the new life you're SUPPOSED to be living was conceived with just a touch from the Holy Ghost, just as with Mary. And from the moment we accepted this assignment – by accepting Jesus Christ as your personal Lord and Savior – we should be working to "BIRTH" Jesus in EVERYTHING we do and say.

Here's the thing – and I'm included in this group: For many of us, the conception part was easy. We had no problem letting God move into our hearts, take up residence and begin to clean our lives up. Yes, there may have been fear of the unknown, some hesitation, but we were sure that He was calling us, and we were going to respond. So, we let God move into our hearts and take up residence. But the birthing part – *that* part for many of us is difficult. We are afraid to let Jesus "come forth" on our job. We're embarrassed to "let our lights" shine at school. We just can't seem to let enough of our flesh die that we let His Spirit in us live. But we have to move past this point. We have to remember, when we were adopted into the family of God, He said to each of us "I want YOU to carry My Son." Will you accept that assignment?

Before you answer that question, can you imagine what the world would be like if Mary had denied this assignment? Salvation, reconciliation, and redemption would be delayed or altogether derailed for us. That's exactly what happens when we deny the assignment to carry His Son. A common sentiment expressed among believers is, "He didn't save you just FOR you. He saved you because He needs you to help reach someone else." My friends, don't think yourselves any less accountable – having any less part – in the will and ultimate plan of God than Mary had. Yes, she was the first one given this assignment, but she was by no means the last. And although you may feel like when you don't allow Jesus to be birthed through you, that it can't possibly be any harm – perhaps because you think you're insignificant in God's plan – DON'T BE FOOLED! You're only delaying or derailing the plan of God. Make the choice to allow Jesus to live through you today.

FROM PAIN TO PRAISE

THE MISCARRIAGE

So...
How do I judge the value of my life?
Money?
Success?
Degrees?
Healthy relationships?
Saved kids?

I work with kids.
Everyday.
I'm in the business of saving them.
From the streets
From disease
From poor choices
From themselves
From uncaring unconcerned parents
From teachers that don't know how to teach
Or how to reach
their fragile selves.

I save kids
Everyday.
But, I couldn't save my own.

I'm riding to Vermont,
One of four adults with twenty kids,
Through the dark, slick, rainy streets
Saying a prayer every hour
For a safe arrival.
For the kids.
A safe arrival
At our destination.
Not knowing
I needed to pray
For my own child's
Safe arrival.
At his,
Or her,
Destination.

I already knew I was bleeding heavy.
From the day before,
Bleeding heavy.
I'm used to bleeding heavy.
But on that bus
To Vermont,
Heavy
Was an understatement.
"It's because you're sitting so long"
A friend says.
Could be.

But not like this.
Changed pad at the last rest stop.
So much blood.
So red.
Smelled so strong.
Now back on the bus,
An hour later,
Feel soaked.
Need to change again.
Then...
Feel clot falling.
Big clot.
Never felt like this before.
Feels like a small ball
Or large egg.
...The irony in it feeling like an egg.
I begin the long walk down the bus aisle
to the bathroom in the back.
Long walk.
Checking kids as I pass.
Checking kids as I pass.
Checking kids as it passes
from cervix
to lips.
Makes me pause in the aisle.
So big.
Why lord?
...I'm checking on the kids.

Bust into bathroom
Slowly peel off pants

There's blood in the crotch
Good jeans… bloodstained.
I think to myself,
"It's only been an hour".
Fear creeps into the already small bathroom,
Takes up the rest of the space.
I reach for my panties
Pull down slowly
Don't know what I'll see
Fear choking me
No air at all now
I see the first of many clots that weekend and start to wonder…
Was it a boy or a girl?
Were you a boy or a girl?
Pick it up with tissue
Hold him/her in the palm of my hand,
Look closer
See real tissue
In there.

I thought I was coming to watch kids
Protect kids
Care for kids
My kid,
My kid…
I had to leave the first part of you in a coach bus toilet.
Wrapped in tissue,
Like a newborn wrapped in blanket.
Didn't even want to throw you away

FROM PAIN TO PRAISE

Wanted to put you in a ziplock bag
Take you to the lab
So I'd know for sure.
But I already knew.
Tossed you away in tissue
Cleaned up
Changed pad
Walked back to seat...
Checking on kids.

I only slept five hours that whole weekend.
Part time chasing kids, making sure they were safe.
Spent every hour in the bathroom flushing blood and tissue down a Vermont toilet.
Spent every other hour changing blood soaked pads, washing underwear,
changing clothes
and flushing more blood and tissue down a Vermont toilet.
Bought a pack of pads before I got on the bus that Friday night.
Had to buy a whole 'nutha fucking pack Sunday afternoon!
Two every other hour!
Two drenched every other hour!
Wings didn't help.
Only served as the wings my child flew to heaven on.
Every wastepaper basket in every bathroom where we stayed housed a piece of what would have been baby,
balled up in sanitary napkins.

And I'm watching kids.

When reality set in as to what was happening, I cried.
For about 3 minutes.
See there was no privacy.
Nowhere to grieve
No time to grieve
Cuz there were kids that needed attention
Kids that needed information
Kids that needed comforting.
So the little energy I did have had to go to them.
So on edge, I snapped at coworkers that weekend.
Kicked
Cursed
Couldn't take part in activities
Cuz every other hour I had to be near a bathroom.
Spoke to kids like I was somebody's mother that weekend.
I had been noticing myself do that a lot during the previous month...
Was that a sign?
Thought I was just being less tolerant,
or more responsible.
But perhaps, instincts were just kicking in.

Depression is what I thought it was.
Anxiety maybe
Or perhaps a devil's attack.
But never did I think pregnancy,
Knowing damn well there was a chance.
September third...

One night only...
Sex,
No condom,
The second time in my whole life I let one enter raw.
Stupid.
Now my child had to pay.
But hey,
Maybe this was justice.
I had spent almost every other night drinking and smoking.
No exercise.
Damn sure not eating right.
So unborn Saunders woulda been fucked anyway
Right?
I don't know
But these are the questions I ask.
These are the doubts that I have.
And this will probably be the only time I take to process this.
Because all this time later,
I'm still
Checking on kids.

GRIEF

I've thought about what to write for a few days.
Staring at the white of the
screen or the blank space of the page,
I realize,
That time is wasting.
Time
is wasting.
I don't have a degree.
Married? No, not me.
Career path mapped out,
But
I just keep straying
And praying
That tomorrow, there'll be more…
Time.
See, this is not the homage I wanted to create.
Not the grief relieving words used to escape
the reality that death is real and can come for anyone
at any

Time.

My thoughts right now are mostly selfish.
I try to think of my old friend.
I try to think of her husband.
I try to think of the child left behind.
And my mind
Can't focus,
Drifts back
To me
My needs, My regrets
My shortcomings, My upsets
In comparison to others, My lack of progress
(I'm always comparing myself to others.)
Not too much though about
how far I HAVE come.
No, this is not the time for celebratory reflection.
Death doesn't illicit that.
It taunts with a flood of regrets.
The focus is on heartbreaks
And the many horrible mistakes
And the moment I drift back to reality
I find my heart losing pace
As if it feels the truth
It knows the truth.
That I am indeed
Running
Out… of Time

UNLOCK GOD'S THOUGHTS TOWARD YOU

For I know the thoughts that I think toward you, saith the LORD, thoughts of peace, and not of evil, to give you an expected end. Then shall ye call upon me, and ye shall go and pray unto me, and I will hearken unto you. And ye shall seek me, and find me, when ye shall search for me with all your heart.
-Jeremiah 29:11-13 (KJV)

For many believers, these are familiar verses of scripture. But I saw them in a new way last night. See, I often seek approval, confirmation and affirmation of who I am from others in my life. Whether it be a friend, family member, church leader, etc... I always seem to need someone else's stamp of approval about a situation in my life. After reading this verse last night, I was a little disgusted with myself. When read in context, we find that these are God's words to the Babylonian captives. He was essentially telling them that they needed to stop listening to the report of all these so-called prophets in their lives. He was telling them that, in all actuality, no one knows HIS thoughts about the situation they were facing EXCEPT for Him. Thus, in this portion of scripture, God was beckoning them to understand that ONLY HE knew what their future held. And this same reminder is needed for us today.

ONLY GOD knows the blueprint for your life. We might turn to friends, family, and trusted leaders for guidance. But guess what? When they've said all they can say... when they've shared their perspectives... ONLY GOD knows what your expected end is. Once we get that through our heads, we have the ultimate privilege, the amazing honor, of coming before Him in Prayer to ask Him about it.

Prayer should be a part of the lifestyle of a Christian. It's not only for making our requests known, or for asking for forgiveness for sins. Our Father, has "thoughts", and He's willing to share them with us. He *wants* to share them with us. Wouldn't you rather know what HE thinks about a situation in your life than anybody else? Think about it. If you're having issues with your car, you could take it to a mechanic for their opinion about it. This is usually helpful. He/she can share what best practices dictate you do to handle the issue with the car. BUT, when you have a one of a kind, no other like it, specialty car, the absolute best person to take it to when unsure about something is the designer himself. You don't let the local mechanic tinker with that car. You take it straight to the creator.

Each of us is one of a kind. Each of us is uniquely designed by God with a purpose in mind. If we're experiencing confusion, trouble, setbacks on this journey, we should be seeking God's thoughts on our lives. He has a plan. And He will give us an expected end.

This is so simple, yet so easy to forget. Seek God and His thoughts. They're the only ones that count. When you remember that He has a plan, you can push all doubt and confusion out of your mind, stop seeking approval from people, and finally search for God with your WHOLE HEART. And you know what? When you do, you will find Him.

STAY ON THE POTTER'S WHEEL

"Go down to the potter's shop, and I will speak to you there." So I did as he told me and found the potter working at his wheel. But the jar he was making did not turn out as he had hoped, so he crushed it into a lump of clay again and started over. Jeremiah 18: 2-4 (NLT)

Daughter... do you know that you are an earthen vessel, filled with heavenly treasure? I first read this beautiful language in 2 Corinthians 4:7. The Lord once gave me a powerful sermon on this topic. It is an AWESOME thought! We are nothing more than jars of clay that God has handcrafted for Himself. We are the work that He, the Potter, is creating on that potter's wheel referenced in the book of Jeremiah.

Take a look at the book of Genesis. There we find

God FORMING Adam out of the dust of the earth. The dust of the earth is clay! He made Adam into a vessel, fit for His service. Then he formed Eve out of a piece of that clay – Adam's rib. She also was made as a vessel, fit for His service. But somewhere along the way, they became marred – damaged. And this is what happens to us. We vessels get damaged in life as well. We get hurt, abused, taken advantage of, talked about, overlooked, cast aside, told that we're not worthy, told that we're ugly. We get marred in this life. Further, paraphrasing what David said in Psalm 51:5, mankind is even conceived and raised in a sinful world. This often causes us to look at ourselves, our circumstances, and our situations and deem ourselves unworthy, or less-than. But just as God showed Jeremiah at the potter's house, the vessels that have been damaged – even those that have been damaged while IN the potter's hand – WILL BE MADE AGAIN! But, this only happens if we stay on the "potter's wheel" – if we continuously allow God to shape and make and mold us as it seems pleasing to HIM!

Daughter, don't give up. This walk isn't easy, but it's worth it. And when you feel you've been "damaged" – whether it was by some sin you committed or at the hands of someone else – you MUST remember that God intends to make you AGAIN! And, AGAIN! And, AGAIN! Stay on the wheel. You are NOT worthless! Stay in His hands. He has use of you! The Potter, the Designer, the Creator – He knows what you've been through. He sees you. And He wants to take you – damage and all - and make you into another vessel! He wants to heal those hurts. He wants you to see yourself as He sees you. He wants to correct your vision. He wants to equip you for purpose. He wants you to access the abundant life He said you could have. He wants you to know that you are His child. His Daughter. So remain on the Potter's wheel. Remain in God's hand. Remain a Daughter-in-Process. I can tell you first-hand that it is worth it.

FOR EVERY MOUNTAIN (MY TESTIMONY)

    I could talk for hours about how awesome God is. I could share countless accounts of the times that He's done something miraculous for me. And when it comes to my deliverance experience, even after so many years, I look back with awe, humility, and near-disbelief at how mightily God moved in my life. Given all of this, I'm ashamed to admit that I haven't shared this testimony more often. I've allowed fear, false humility, and sometimes even shame to keep me from doing so on many occasions. And if I'm really honest, sometimes, I just don't think people will believe me. My life was so drastically different before He delivered me that when people look at who I am today, oftentimes they can't fathom that I ever had a drinking problem, or was an adulterer, or that I ever picked up a cigarette or a blunt a day in my life. And aside from fear of disbelief, there was also a fear of judgement. Some people can't stand to hear that the woman that just prayed down heaven at the church conference used to be a loose woman. They might not accept the message being delivered by the messenger. I didn't want to be a stumbling block to anyone. But when it came to writing this book, I could not fight the Holy Ghost on including my testimony. I tried. Believe me, I tried. I attempted to go to print so many times without including a retelling of my deliverance experience. But He just wouldn't let me. So here, unable to hold it back any longer, I will share my testimony..

I was not a churched youth. Nor was I raised in a Christian home. However, I was by no means a stranger to God or church. I had several family members come pick me up on sporadic Sunday mornings to join them for church service. And as a child, my grandmother and mother did make me get down on my knees at bedtime to recite the "Now I Lay Me Down to Sleep" prayer. I even went to a Christian sleep-away summer camp between the ages of 8 and 10. And it was at this camp that I first accepted Christ as my personal Lord and Savior. I was about 8 or 9 years old. It happened during one-on-one cabin devotion time. My camp counselor and I were sitting on a blanket on the grassy hill outside of our cabin. I don't remember the topic of devotion that day, but the Holy Spirit must have prompted her to share Christ with me, and she did. I remember crying as I learned about this Jesus that loved me, and that died for me. She saw this, and offered to lead me in the prayer of salvation. I wholeheartedly agreed. And as soon as I said the words "I accept You as Lord and Savior. I ask you to come into my heart", I felt a cool chill spread across my chest. It felt like a spring of cool water had burst over my heart. It was beautiful. It was cleansing. I cried. Even my child's mind understood that I had somehow, in the moment, been changed. I have never forgotten that day. I returned home that summer a true Believer. However, not being churched, I was not discipled, and never really developed my relationship with Christ. But, when I look back on my life, I realize that God made a way for me to stay in fellowship with Him every step of the way. And His main vehicle to do so was school.

At the age of 10, I ended up going to a Catholic middle school. From there, I went to a Catholic high school. And although I do not practice Catholicism, there was something to be said about religious schools. In middle school I had religious instruction daily, prayed daily, and went to religious services weekly. High school was similar. The school had annual spiritual retreats, special religious services, a caring campus minister, Christmas and Resurrection celebrations (in their true Christian context), and I believe that ALL of this was God's way of keeping me close to Him, even though I was not actively seeking Him on my own. However, these protective environments had another consequence of leaving me jaded about the world around me. And when I graduated from high school, although I never abandoned my faith, I began a slow, yet steady, downward spiral into the things of the world, losing myself in the process. Ultimately, things got so bad, that if God had not stepped in, I am sure – HEAR ME CLEARLY – I am SURE that I would be dead.

Now, I hate to rush through the next 10 years of my life. But to explain each and every level of decent down the ladder of destruction that I took would turn this into a memoir, and not a testimony. So I'll just list some of the most significant experiences along my downward spiral. These are some of the events that propelled me deeper and deeper into pain, most of which I lived in silence. Between the ages of 18 and 27, several things happened:
- ✓ The occasional cigarette I started out with at the age of 15 intensified into a pack-a-day habit.
- ✓ At around age 19 I began smoking weed.
- ✓ That same year, I dropped out of college (for the first of many times).
- ✓ I also then fell into my first depression.
- ✓ At my 21st birthday party, a family friend – in a drug induced rage – put my and my mom's life in danger by brandishing a knife in an attempt to stab one of my party guests, leaving me slightly traumatized – especially since this family friend lived with us.
- ✓ A few months after the birthday party fiasco, I was sexually assaulted by a stranger on a

NYC train during the work day. I went back to work like nothing had happened. And when I was ready, I only told 4 friends.
- ✓ Later that same year, I was sexually assaulted by a friend.
- ✓ The trauma associated with the above three incidents led to post traumatic stress disorder and hypervigilance that led to the development of Panic Disorder and clinical depression. I had to quit my job and move out of my mom's house. (I moved back in a year later.)
- ✓ As a result of the experiences with sexual assault, I was then afraid that if I didn't give up my virginity soon, someone would take it from me. I had intended to save it for marriage – or at last real love. I remember literally feeling like the devil was after my virginity. It just seemed as if I was bound to get raped one day. So, I decided to give up my virginity before someone took it. I lost it to a friend at the age of 21.
- ✓ Although therapy and medication helped the Panic Disorder and depression greatly, I had also learned to self-medicate. Alcohol became my best friend by the age of 23. It helped with the social and general anxiety I still dealt with from time to time. And it helped to drown out my poor self-image and low self-esteem. When I was drunk, I was the life of the party!
- ✓ Somewhere around the age of 23, I also

started to experiment with bisexuality. And having such a low self-image, I began to settle for sexual relationships with men that didn't really love me (and whom I also didn't love). Some of these men were in relationships, and at least one was married.

✓ Between the ages of 23 and 26 I went from being an occasional drinker, to a weekend drinker, to an everyday drinker, to an everyday drinker that got drunk to the point of blackout on Thursday, Friday *and* Saturday. Yes, I became a full blown functional alcoholic. There were days I woke up in strange places, or with bumps or bruises I couldn't recall getting. One night I remember my good friend having to come find me in the street, scoop me up off the curb where I was passed out (after a cab driver abandoned me there), and take me home.

I – Was – Miserable. I wanted a change, but I didn't know how to get it. My biggest hurdle was the alcohol. I could barely go a day without drinking. And if I didn't slow down, I was going to end up putting myself into increasingly dangerous situations. Then, at the age of 26, God set the wheels in motion for all of this to change.

In 2007 I was 26 years old and working at a job that was dysfunctional in its own ways. But there was a group of young women there who happened to be

Christians, one of whom was a very old friend of mine. (Throughout this testimony, I'll call her "Prayer Warrior".) I was busy running with the crew at work that drank and partied like I did. But little did I know that this group of women was enjoying a different type of fellowship with each other. Little by little I was drawn into their conversations about God and faith. Through my interactions with them, God was pulling me back to Him, although I didn't know it at the time. Then, by mid-2007, one of these women (I'll call her "Prophet") was talking about feeling led by God to host a women's retreat to Arizona. To prepare for this, she hosted a series of fellowships leading up to this retreat. I took part in all of it, loving every minute of it, although I was still partying hard. My time with these ladies was the bit of light I needed to shine in all the darkness I was dealing with – and getting tired of. Something was nudging me to go on this retreat. And so I did.

My First Mountain

In March of 2008, I and six other young women embarked on this retreat to Sedona, AZ. I was 27 years old by then. The retreat's theme was "Taking Back Your Authority". I'll never forget the morning I left. As I prepared to leave my house to catch my flight, something in me was disturbed. I began to cry. I thought I was being overly emotional. But "something" told me that I would not be coming back. What did that mean? I actually entertained the thought that perhaps I would not survive this trip.

(That was nothing but fear tormenting me.) But that wasn't it. My spirit-man understood. I remember wiping the tears from eyes, breathing heavily, closing the door behind me and walking away, knowing I would not be coming back the same way I was leaving. There was something I was taking with me, that I would not be bringing back. I didn't know what to expect, but I was ready.

On our first full day in Sedona, we set out for the buttes (hills). Now, being from the city, we called these buttes *mountains*. (They were bigger than any hills we had ever seen.) They were large, red colored, mountainous formations, which were frequented by tourists. However, on this day, they weren't particularly crowded by any means. So we arrived at the foot of the mountains, and climbed out of our SUV not knowing what to expect. But Prophet had a plan. The entire itinerary was filled with activities that she said the Lord wanted us to do. We quickly learned that our first activity would be a trust walk. Prophet blindfolded all of us, had us line up and hold on to the shoulders of the person in front of us, and then led us up the side of the mountain. As we ascended, I was filled with a range of feelings – mostly anger and confusion. As far as I was concerned, this was inappropriate. I didn't sign up for this! I was a smoker. I was heavy. I fatigued quicker than the rest of the ladies. I felt like whoever was ahead of me wasn't really making sure I was keeping up. I felt way too vulnerable… and unsafe. It was the longest 5 minute walk of my life.

Once we got to a broad landing that seemed high enough, we stopped. We were then lined up side by side, told to remove our blindfolds and to look out at the majesty and glory of God. We did. I stood there, looking out at an absolutely beautiful scene. But my heart had been hardened on the walk up, so I couldn't enjoy it. In fact, I refused to enjoy it. While the rest of the ladies scattered and went into some private praise and worship, I sulked. I heard them saying things like "Hallelujah" and "God You're amazing". I, however, refused to be impressed. Yes, the view was breathtaking, but I was still *literally* out of breath, sweating heavily, and angry from the trust walk. I didn't want to see "God's glory" – whatever that meant. I wanted an explanation as to what the heck that trust walk was all about! I wanted to sit down somewhere! I wanted a cigarette! I wanted a drink!

While the rest of the ladies began to roam around and have their own private worship moments with God, I continued to sulk. A short while later Prophet began walking over to each lady, holding their hands, and prophesying to them. Once again, I was ignorant as to what was happening. I didn't fully understand prophecy. But I remember her coming to me and taking my hands. I closed my eyes like I had seen some of the others do, but she quickly released my hands and withdrew from me, almost as if I had shocked her. She said "Hmm… You're not ready.

You're too angry. I'll come back to you in a bit." I opened my eyes and saw a true look of concern on her face. My heart softened a little. So I leaned up against a perch on the mountainside and watched her continue to work with the others. Then, I saw that our semi-private moment was about to be interrupted. Two women speaking to each other in some Russian-type of language came walking by. I thought, "Uh-oh! They're gonna think we're crazy." At that very moment, Prophet was loudly praying with one of the ladies. I was embarrassed for us. I watched to see what was about to happen. (No one else seemed concerned.) Prophet walked away from the young lady she was praying with and began walking in the general direction of the two women approaching our area. Then Prophet locked eyes with one of the women. They walked directly up to one another. The woman grabbed Prophet's hands, just as she had been grabbing our hands. That was shocking enough. But then I *really* couldn't believe what happened next. The Russian woman began to speak in English to Prophet, prophesying to her! My mind was blown! I didn't understand what I was witnessing. Did this foreign woman just switch languages? I know I'm making the assumption that this woman didn't know English at all. But whether she did or did not, it still didn't explain how she was drawn to Prophet and able to prophesy about her life! I had never witnessed an encounter like that. Was this a set-up? I was the newbie in the group. Was I being set up??? I did not yet know the many ways in which God works. This could not be real! I listened to this woman minister to Prophet about her situation. As she ended, she gave her a charge of some sort, which caused Prophet to fall to her knees with a loud moan. The woman let go of Prophet's hands, then turned to walk back towards her friend whom had held back a bit while she worked. Prophet was left on the ground, down on all fours, breathing heavily with tears in her eyes as she stared after Russian woman in awe. Then, as they walked by, I will never forget how they both looked me in my eyes. My heart was completely softened at that point. I wanted something too. Everybody was getting something, experiencing something. I wanted an experience too! Prophet was in her own glory cloud at that moment. So I looked around and saw that another one of the ladies with us was climbing a bit higher up the mountain. I wasn't the explorer type, but I decided to climb a little higher too, and see what I would find. I was in search of an experience with God. And boy, did I find one.

I climbed a bit further up the side of the mountain, not knowing what I was looking for. But I knew when I saw it. It was a little perch that jutted out like a short stool. There was a bush that hung over it, almost like a personal canopy. It appeared to be a seat, placed there just for me. It practically welcomed me, as there was no one else around. So I sat on that perch. And I looked out at the horizon. And I saw God. I finally allowed myself to really take in His Glory. The sky had never seemed so blue in all my life. The air never felt so clean. The sun had never been more perfectly golden – not overbearing and hot… just big, bright and beautiful. I saw God. And then I heard Him. Never before had I heard the audible voice of God. He said "Look down". I looked down and saw a rock. It was almost triangular in shape. It looked flawed, especially amongst all that beauty. I picked it up, and I heard Him say "That's you." I laughed and thought, "What?" He said "That's you. Rough around the edges… Worn from the elements… flawed." I became sad at the thought of my rough edges… my flaws. I held the rock in my hand and sat in silence for a few moments. Then I heard Him speak again, "Look down." I saw another rock. I picked it up. It was almost perfectly round, much smoother – not perfect, just better than the first one. He said "This is what I will do with you. I will smooth out your rough edges. The closer you get to me, the more perfect you'll become. You won't be perfect. Only I Am perfect. But you will become more perfect the closer you get to me. I will remove those flaws." I smiled. Not perfect, but better. I thought, "I'll take it." I held the rocks in my hand and stared out at the horizon for a few more moments. I smiled broadly. I had just heard the voice of God, and I was SURE it was Him! I was in His presence, and it felt amazing! He took time to talk directly to ME!

I began my descent back down to the group.

When I did, I heard one of the ladies (I'll call her Big Sis) scream up to me, "Inacent!"
"Yea? I'm coming now!" I said.
"No! He said hang out with Him!"
Pause
"What?" I asked.
"God... He said to tell you to stay there and hang out with Him."
I chuckled a little bit and began to climb back up. When I got to my perch and sat down, I cynically asked "Okay God, what do we do when we 'hang out'?"
"DON'T MOCK ME!" responded the Voice of God. I shrank back. I was afraid in that moment. I learned a quick lesson in reverencing the Lord. He continued on, "You don't even know HOW to hang out anymore! Remember *that*? Just 'hanging out'???"
It was sharp. It cut deep. And He was right. My mind flooded with memories from my teenaged years, when my friends and I would just "hang out". A bottle of liquor wasn't necessary. Drugs and cigarettes weren't necessary. Maybe we'd watch a movie, order a pizza, do our hair, talk about life and relationships, laugh at each other, talk about people (not the best activity, but standard for teenaged girls), play cards, put on our favorite music and dance with each other, go for walks all over Brooklyn... I cried. Those days were gone. Hanging out now meant popping bottles, going to the bar or club, smoking blunts, going home with somebody for a meaningless romp. God was right. I didn't know how to just

"hang out" anymore. I was saddened again.

Then, God's voice gently broke the silence. "Hang out with Me. I will show you things Inacent. Things you never thought you'd see. You'll do things you never thought you'd do. I'll smooth your rough edges. You won't be perfect, but you'll be better. I'll strip away your flaws. The closer you get to me, the better you'll become. Hang out with me." I cried, and cried. It was a cleansing cry. I looked out again at the beauty of the sky, the mountains, the clouds, the trees… the Creator of all of that wanted me to hang out with Him. I needed that rebuke from the Lord. When I attempted to go back down the mountain the first time, He had to turn me around and make sure that I understood what He was saying about getting closer to Him. He had to break it down in terms I understood. My friends and I are only still friends to this day because of that time spent in our teen years – "hanging out" and getting to know each other, without all that extra stuff. That's what God wanted with me. And I knew in that moment that I badly wanted it with Him.

After a short while I began my descent down the mountain again. Big Sis was the first person I encountered on my way down. "Inacent! You're glowing! Oh my goodness, look at your face! What happened up there?" I had no idea what she was talking about. I kept smiling and walking down the mountain. I think I said something smart like "I was hanging out with God, like you told me to!" She kept going on and on. "Look at her face! She looks totally different!" When we encountered some of the other ladies, they had the same reaction. I was ignorant at the time to what being in God's presence can do to one's appearance. I wasn't familiar with the full story of Moses. But apparently, my countenance had changed. God had spoken. And it was only day two. I didn't believe that anything greater could happen. But with God, there's always more.

My Second Mountain

The next day we set out for the Chapel of the Holy Cross. This chapel, built into the side of the hills in Sedona, was a popular tourist destination. As we walked up the long winding hill to the chapel, I was once again in awe of the beauty of God's creation. And as we walked, I had a song playing in my head that I had heard for the first time the previous night during our praise and worship session. It was called "When the Saints Go to Worship". Somehow I knew that I was in for the worship experience of a lifetime.

Once again, when we got to the top of the hill where the entrance to the chapel was, everyone seemed to scatter and do their own thing. So I went and sat in the chapel. I remember being disgusted that there was so much talking and meaningless chatter going on. Although it was a tourist spot, I felt like there should have been more respect for the fact that this was indeed a sanctuary. I tried my best to block the noise out and hear from God again. Maybe He would speak like He did the day before. He did speak, but this time the voice seemed to come from within myself. He said, "Take off your shoes." I almost laughed, because I immediately remembered the story of Moses and the burning bush. My first thought was "Take off my shoes? I'm no Moses!" But I remembered the lesson I learned about mocking God the day before. So instead I talked to myself, saying "Take off my shoes? Here? For *what*? These people are gonna look at me like I'm crazy!" So I just sat there. Then I heard it again. "Take off your shoes." Ugh! I let a few moments pass, then I slipped off my sneakers and slid them neatly under the pew I was sitting on. I sat there a few moments more and thought to myself "Ok, now what?" "Go outside", He said. I was dumbfounded. I was supposed to leave the chapel in only my socks? Why? None of this made sense.

I eventually worked up the courage to walk back outside in just my socks. As I exited the chapel, I looked up, and my eyes fell upon a distinctive white shape on the side of the red mountain in front of me. What intrigued me about it was that it was in the shape of a fish. I remembered from Catholic school that one of the symbols that represented Jesus in the early church was that of a fish. Was it real? Was I making something out of nothing? I mean, it was so distinct that it almost looked like it had been intentionally placed there – perhaps by the architect of the chapel. In any event, I continued to walk, slightly bewildered, while looking up at this fish. Suddenly, I began to feel as if I was being pulled. I mean, *really* pulled… like a magnetic pull. My feet were moving but I felt like I was getting dragged by something… like something bigger than me had grabbed me by my shirt and was steering me in a particular direction. That's how strong it was. I felt like I was being steered. I passed one of my roommates on the way (I'll call her Roommate), and she looked at me and said "Where are you going?" I couldn't even look at her as the fish-shaped rock was still captivating me. I simply mumbled "I don't know."

I felt crazy. First, I heard a voice tell me to take off my shoes in public. Then, I felt like I wasn't in control of where I was going. Eventually the steering stopped and that same force literally sat me down on the ledge that lined the walkway that led up to the chapel entrance. I then heard the voice of God again. He said "Lay down." My heart began to beat a little faster with that. That ledge was all that separated the walkway up to the chapel from a bumpy roll down the mountainside. If I laid on the ledge and rolled over, I'd surely either be badly injured, or possibly dead. In that moment I remembered the feeling I had when I left home – the one that I had in my carnal mind that I might somehow die on this trip. Was that what was happening? Was I about to die? What the *heck* was going on?

Roommate stood watching me. I determined I would do what I was told, but I needed some security. With tears in my eyes I asked, "Roommate, can you come sit next to me?" She looked hesitant but only for a split second. She then came and sat next to me. When she did, I scooted over some and stretched out along the ledge on my back. "What are you doing?" she asked. "I don't know." I replied. So I laid there fighting back tears. After a few moments, I took a chance of looking over the edge of the mountain. I almost jumped at what I saw. It was a rock in the distinct shape of two tablets. Yes, tablets like the ones we usually see depicting the Ten Commandments. (I later learned that I was having a vision for the very first time.) I was immediately calmed, yet also amazed! "God, what is that?!" I asked in my mind.
"A covenant." He replied.
"A covenant?"
"Yes. A covenant. From this day on, you will be my child, and I will be your God."
"Yes.", I wholeheartedly agreed. There was something about the way He said "…your God", that immediately made me realize how personal this relationship was to be. I would no longer have to access God through others. Just like I was hearing Him clearly for myself on this trip, I would continue to hear from Him – as well as freely speak to Him. He was no longer just God, but He was now *my* God.

I closed my eyes and thought about that for a

moment. *My* God. I opened my eyes again, and looked back towards where the tablets had been. When I looked, I saw a rock – something more like a huge boulder. But it looked like it was hanging onto the side of the mountain by just the tiniest piece of rock. It was bound to fall off. Still not understanding that I was in the middle of a vision, I felt like I was about to witness some natural catastrophe… like the mountains were about to crumble, if even only in the area where I was looking. But that boulder was hanging on for dear life! I blinked a few times not able to believe what I was seeing. I asked in my mind "God, what *is* that?"

He said, "Remember when I said you had some flaws on you that I was going to remove… in order to perfect you?"

"Yes."

"Well that's what that rock is. Those flaws – the things I want to break off of you. Just like that rock looks like it's ready to break away from the mountain, you're flaws are ready to be broken off of you. That's what I'm going to do. I'm going to break them off of you." I began to cry. That's all that I wanted. To be freed from those things that I couldn't seem to shake on my own… the things that were tormenting me – killing me. Still crying, I asked, "When, God?"

He said, "Right NOW!"

In that moment my body began to shake. Not like a seizure. But it rocked back and forth as I laid on the ledge. The rocking was emanating from somewhere in my very core. My crying intensified. I felt something welling up in my chest. I felt like I needed to scream. But I fought that urge. I didn't want to cause a scene. And once again, I didn't understand what was happening. Roommate saw what was happening and immediately stood up. She began to scream at me. "Let it go! Let it go! Whatever it is, let it GO! Don't swallow it! Let it out!" I clenched my eyes tightly. I breathed heavily, with deep throaty moans. I sounded nothing like myself. I didn't know what she wanted me to do.

Suddenly, I felt someone touching my forehead. I thought it was Roommate. Then I heard a male's voice saying "The blood of Jesus. The blood of Jesus. The blood of Jesus." He said it over and over. I opened my eyes to see an older white gentleman with his hand on my forehead. I only point out that he was white because that seemed to add to my anxiety at the time. Being among only a handful of black people there, I didn't want the white people starting at the "loud, crazy, black girl". I breathed heavier and as I opened my mouth that time, a noise of anguish came out. I closed my eyes in confusion and embarrassment, and then opened them again. I allowed my eyes to roll around to look at the passersby. Were they staring? Oh great! I had an audience – or at least it felt like I did. I closed my eyes again. The man was still pleading the "blood of Jesus". I was busy trying to fight whatever this feeling was welling up in side of me. I didn't want to cause a scene. But then something happened. In my mind's eye, I saw something that looked like a vapor of a hand descend from the sky. This large hand reached inside of me, grabbed hold of the tightness in my chest, and pulled it out. And as it pulled, I opened my mouth and heard a scream come out. It wasn't my own voice. It was a scream of anguish, a horrible scream. It was the scream of demons coming out of me. The tears continued to flow and my body continued to shake until the scream came to an end. I laid there crying and breathing heavily. The man and Roommate began to praise God. Then he told me to sit up. He said "Sister, you've been delivered! You've been delivered from whatever you were dealing with. I don't know what it was. But know that God has delivered you! He has set you free. Do you believe that?"

I shook my head up and down through sobs.

He said "Good. Now, you have to renounce everything that He just delivered you from. Whatever it is, out of your own mouth, I want you to say 'I renounce it in the name of Jesus!'"

"I renounce it in the name of Jesus." I whimpered.

He said "No, say it like you mean it. And what is it you're renouncing? Call it by name. Is it abuse? Is it drugs? Call it out by name!"

So there, on that mountainside in Sedona, Arizona, I declared out of my own mouth:

"I renounce fornication, in the name of Jesus!
I renounce alcoholism, in the name of Jesus!

I renounce drugs, in the name of Jesus!
I renounce depression, in the name of Jesus!
I renounce the sexual perversion, in the name of Jesus!
I renounce the cigarettes, in the name of JESUS!"
When I was done running down the list, and when the crying slowed down some, I realized that I felt 30 pounds lighter. I had been delivered from every tempting, controlling, manipulating, spirit of addiction, lust, and fear that I was dealing with. God even took the taste for alcohol and cigarettes out of my mouth. The very smell of them became repulsive to me. I had been set free!

I am fully persuaded that if God had not stepped in when He did, I very well may not be alive today. Any number of things could have happened to me. One of the next times I got drunk and blacked out, I may have never awakened. The next time I found myself in some drunken stupor, I could have fell down and cracked my head open. The next time I passed out in the street, it could have been a stranger that scooped me up and took me home – or the cab driver may have decided to have a party of his own with me. I may have contracted some sexually transmitted infection the next time I thought I could sleep with some other woman's boyfriend, or anyone for that matter! The devil definitely had a plan for my life to end in tragedy. But God had a greater purpose! I indeed returned home as a completely different person than when I had left. And the glory that was

revealed in my countenance, was seen by others when I got home. Do you understand me? The change was so thorough, it was visible! As soon as I saw some of my friends and family they said things like:
"You don't even have to say nothing. I can tell you're not the same."
"So no more partying, huh?"
"I'm just gonna let you do you. I know you can't hang out with me no more."
The change was so dramatic, Big Sis referred to me as Paul after that, because I had been so drastically changed by my encounter with God, and became so passionate about growing in Christ. Grace and mercy have kept me in these things from 2008 to today! I am literally a living testimony.

I wish I could say that I avoided all of these things for the rest of my walk with God. But temptation did come, and it still does come. In fact, after this unbelievable, life-changing experience, temptation came the very next day. And I gave in.

My Third Mountain
Now, usually when I do share my testimony, I leave out the part I'm about to share. It doesn't always serve the listener well to hear this part. Most times they just need to hear about God's power to save, heal and set free. But this part is relevant, especially for the purposes of this book – about being a Daughter in Process. See, although I was

delivered from all matter of sin that day, I did not have a full understanding of what it meant to be delivered from sinful habits. So although I had thrown away the pack of cigarettes I had with me after my deliverance experience, it was going to take more than that to *stay* delivered. No one had explained that to me. So the very next day when the enemy tempted me, I gave in to temptation. Thus began a crash course in maintaining my deliverance.

The day after my second mountain experience, the seven of us had breakfast together. Now, any smoker will tell you that a cigarette following a meal is almost a requirement. So after I finished my meal, although I didn't have the desire for a cigarette, I did have a desire to fulfill that post meal ritual. So of course, the devil brought to my remembrance the fact that I had a cigarette clip left in the ashtray out on my hotel room balcony from a day or two before. Yes, this is how crafty the enemy is. He didn't have me go buy a pack of cigarettes. He led me to a tiny, half smoked clip that I had abandoned days ago. I thought "It can't possibly do too much harm to just smoke that little piece of cigarette. I'll smoke it, get it out my system, and be done with smoking forever after that." But the devil is a liar! I had no need to go back to that clip. I wasn't hard pressed for a cigarette. But I surely left the breakfast table and went back to my room like a fiend to smoke that cigarette clip.

When I got to the room, I sat down on that

balcony, picked up that cigarette clip, lit it, and took one pull expecting to feel my last fulfilling post-meal nicotine rush! Instead, I fell out on the floor, doubled over on my knees, holding my chest, and coughing in pain. I thought I was going to die – again! The smoke filled my lungs and it burned! I crumpled up on the floor of that balcony not understanding what was happening. You would have thought I'd never smoked a day in my life! It was as if my lungs were not used to 12 years of smoking! Little did I know that God had also healed me of all damage done to my body due to drinking and smoking. I had truly been made new! So it was indeed as if I had never smoked a day in my life. In any event, I put the cigarette out, ran inside to drink some water (like that would help) and collapsed on the bed, dizzy, with a headache, and a burning chest. I began to cry – again. I repented right away. Prayer Warrior and Roommate came to the room and found me on the bed. I embarrassingly told them what had happened. They then began to explain deliverance to me and what I should have done when I was tempted. (Resist the enemy so he would flee!) I learned the lesson. But since I had foolishly turned back to cigarettes, if even just for that one pull, God had to do a little bit more work on me. And it would take place on our last day there, as we visited one last mountain.

This mountain was not beautiful like the others. It was quite desolate. There wasn't much greenery. There was no view of the blue sky and bright sun. In fact, it felt much more like a valley. It simply wasn't pretty at all. There were no tourists. We were alone. Frankly, it was a bit scary. And, I don't quite remember the word Prophet delivered to us on this mountain. But it was more of a cautionary one than the others were. We ended by closing out in prayer. Then, mid-prayer she began to prophesy to me about maintaining my deliverance. The words were harsh. I honestly don't remember them all. But what I do remember is when she lunged at me and laid her hand on my head, causing me to fall backwards and hit my head on a rock. She landed on top of me and began to scream "You will NEVER smoke another cigarette again. NEVER!" Of course, I began to cry again. Not just for the strong rebuke, but also because I couldn't move with her on top of me, and I DISTINCTLY felt like something was oozing out of my head. Yes, I thought she had cracked my head open on that rock. I just knew I was bleeding to death. Yes, once again, thoughts of an untimely death returned again. When the Spirit lifted, she got up from on top of me, and I was helped up by the other ladies. I rubbed the back of my head to feel the blood that I *knew* had to be there. There was nothing. What did I feel oozing out? (One of the ladies later said to me that it may have been spiritual. That perhaps the last remnants of whatever spirits were tormenting my mind were being expelled. It made sense in a way. If on the second mountain, I felt the hand of God reach into my heart to uproot some things, perhaps this time He was releasing something from my mind.)

In any event, we left this mountain and were told prophetically to shake the dust of our feet, and to not collect any mementos from this place as we had at our other stops on this trip. We went back to our SUV to set out on our journey back to New York. I've been walking with the Lord ever since. And the rest is history.

As I said, I wanted to be sure to include this part of my testimony because there may be some Daughters reading this that need to understand that being in relationship with God is an ongoing process. He can, and will, meet you WHEREVER you are, even at what feels like your lowest point in life. And He will personally journey with you to bring you into greater and greater realms of perfection. Sometimes, people (especially church people) make us feel like we have to be perfect for God to love us. But that's not the case! God's love is unconditional. The true desire of His heart is to be back in relationship with you. That's all He wanted from Adam in the Garden of Eden. When Adam sinned, he lost fellowship with God. And that's what sin does to us – it separates us from God. But God is not scared of your sin. God is concerned with your soul! He wants your soul to be set free so you can worship Him, grow with Him, journey with Him, love with Him, and become AT ONE WITH Him. That's what this process is about. Growing in relationship with God. Discovering your identity in Jesus Christ. Knowing that you are a Daughter of the King! Do you know who you are?

God is calling out to you, just like He did to Adam when He cried out in the Garden, "Adam, where are you?" God is looking for His Daughters today. He wants to declare to someone "You will be my child. And I will be your God!" Say "yes" today. Say "YES" to deliverance. Say "YES" to restoration. Say "YES" to the process. Yours may not look like mine, and that's okay. But Daughter, I implore you, embrace your process! It's time... It's time to turn your pain into praise!

ABOUT THE AUTHOR

Inacent Saunders was born and raised in Brooklyn, NY. She first accepted Christ into her life at the age of 8. However, being an unchurched youth, during her adolescent years she gave in to the temptations of the world and began a downward spiral of destructive behavior that left her dealing with anxiety and depression, and living a life submitted to the lusts of the flesh. Inacent didn't truly start living for Christ until a life-changing encounter with God at age 27. Her testimony of deliverance and redemption is evidence of God's power to change lives. Since being born again, she has allowed the Lord to use her in many ways.

In response to the prompting of God to equip and encourage young believers in a way that she herself had not been, in 2009 Inacent founded *Timothy's Tribe*, a faith-based nonprofit association whose mission is to help teens and young adults discover and walk in their identities in Christ. She has also been invited to preach at special services, and facilitate workshops for young women at conferences. A Certified Youth Chaplain and a powerful prayer warrior, Inacent serves as the Co-Administrator of her church's prayer team. She faithfully devotes her time and resources to the upkeep of the Kingdom of God.

Professionally, Inacent works as the Program Director for an HIV education organization serving young people in NYC. She has been a dedicated youth-worker and nonprofit professional for more than 15 years, serving in various areas of youth development including sexuality education, gang prevention, and leadership development. *From Pain to Praise* is her first published work. For more information visit www.inacentsaunders.com.

www.ingramcontent.com/pod-product-compliance
Lightning Source LLC
Chambersburg PA
CBHW022135080426
42734CB00006B/369